DATE DUE

W9-AFG-377

CULTURES OF THE WORLD

BANGLADESH

Mariam Whyte

MARSHALL CAVENDISH
New York • London • Sydney

Reference edition published 1999 by
Marshall Cavendish Corporation
99 White Plains Road
Tarrytown
New York 10591

© Times Editions Pte Ltd 1999

Originated and designed by
Times Books International, an imprint of
Times Editions Pte Ltd

Printed in Malaysia

Library of Congress Cataloging-in-Publication Data:

Whyte, Mariam.
    Bangladesh / Mariam Whyte.
      p. cm.—(Cultures of the World)
    Includes bibliographical references and index.
    Summary: Describes the geography, history, government,
economy, people, religion, language, arts, leisure, festivals,
and food of Bangladesh.
    ISBN 0-7614-0869-X (library binding)
    1. Bangladesh—Juvenile literature. [1. Bangladesh]
I. Title. II. Series.
DS393.4.W49   1999
954.92—dc21   98–22428
           CIP
           AC

INTRODUCTION

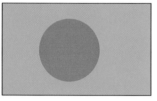

BANGLADESH IS ONE of the world's youngest nations. Historically it has been part of India and has been reborn twice, once as Pakistan and again as Bangladesh. Bangladeshis fought for many years to gain their independence, first to protect their religion, then to protect their language. Today the country is still fighting, this time to achieve a government that can translate their aspirations into reality.

Bangladesh is overpopulated and impoverished, and the journey to economic stability has been slowed again and again by political turmoil. Torrential floods regularly wash through the predominantly wet land, creating still more problems. The people of Bangladesh are, however, enormously proud of their country, and these struggles have not dampened their spirits. Instead they have worked to enrich their culture and to instill a strong national identity.

CONTENTS

A farmer is almost hidden by his heavy load of jute fibers.

CONTENTS

A girl with her water pot.

GEOGRAPHY

BANGLADESH, WHICH IS LOCATED IN SOUTHERN ASIA, is bordered by Burma (Myanmar) to the southeast and India to the west, north, and northeast. Of its total land boundary of 2,637 miles (4,246 km), about 120 miles (193 km) of border is shared with Burma and the rest with India. Bangladesh also has about 360 miles (580 km) of coastline overlooking the Bay of Bengal.

The country covers 55,598 square miles (144,000 square km), an area slightly smaller than Wisconsin. However, due to the overwhelming flatness of the land and the heavy monsoons that blow through each year, bringing heavy rain, a large portion of the country is permanently flooded.

Opposite: **Rice fields in the Ganges Delta. After relying on the monsoon rains for centuries, some farmers have begun to use irrigation systems.**

Left: **The road to Jessore in western Bangladesh.**

Bangladesh's highest peak, the Keokradong (3,041 feet/927 m), is found in the Chittagong Hill Tracts in the southeast of the country.

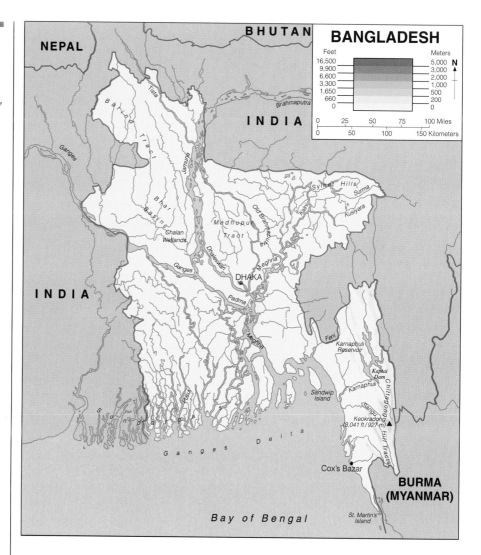

WEB OF RIVERS

An extensive and intricate web of rivers is Bangladesh's most significant geographical feature. The rivers have been a major factor in shaping life and culture in Bangladesh. With over 118 inches (300 cm) of snow and rainfall annually, the eastern Himalayas to the north of Bangladesh provide a major water supply to the Ganges/Brahmaputra/Meghna river systems that empty into the Bay of Bengal.

A boat plies one of Bangladesh's many rivers.

The rivers bring down the rich alluvial soil that forms the Ganges Delta, and they provide the principal means of transportation throughout the country. Rivers are also a source of hydroelectric power, a notable example being the Karnaphuli River in the southeast. Because the rivers are subject to constant and often rapid change, Bangladesh's topography never remains the same for long.

A classic example of this occurred in 1787 when the Tista River experienced massive flooding. Waters were diverted eastward where they met with and reinforced the Brahmaputra River. The swollen Brahmaputra then cut into a minor stream and by the early 1800s the minor stream had become the river's main watercourse, now called the Jamuna. The Brahmaputra, now a considerably smaller river below the juncture with the Jamuna, still flows along the old course.

Lush tropical vegetation covers the Chittagong Hills.

CHITTAGONG HILL TRACTS

Bangladesh has virtually no mountains. The highest elevations in the country are in the southeast, in the Chittagong Hill Tracts. Here some hills rise to more than 2,000 feet (600 m), but the area is atypical of Bangladesh's topography.

Bangladesh's Chittagong Hill Tracts area is just a small section of a much larger mountain range that stretches from west Burma to the eastern Himalayas in China. The steep jungle hills, ravines, and cliffs that are found here are a stark contrast to the flat plains in the rest of Bangladesh.

Unlike the rest of Bangladesh, the Chittagong Hill Tracts area has a relatively low population density. These hills are home to the indigenous peoples collectively known as the Jumma.

The Sylhet region in the northeast is Bangladesh's only other hilly area. Some parts of these hills, which range from 100 to 800 feet (30 to 240 m) high, are covered with forests of bamboo.

THE LONGEST BEACH IN THE WORLD

The beaches along Bangladesh's southeast coast near Cox's Bazar is the longest continuous stretch of beaches in the world, extending over 74 miles (120 km). At high tide the beaches are over 650 feet (200 m) wide; at low tide this width can extend to 1,300 feet (400 m).

Running parallel to the beaches for the entire length of the coast are the forests of the Chittagong Hill Tracts, making the area one of the most picturesque in all of Bangladesh.

SUNDARBANS

The Sundarbans are a massive area of littoral mangrove and jungle found in the southwest of the country on the Ganges Delta, bordering the Bay of Bengal. Covering an area of about 3,860 square miles (10,000 square km), this belt of forest, the largest of its type in the world, stretches over Indian and Bangladeshi territory.

Almost half of the Sundarbans lies under water. The low-lying alluvial islands, mudbanks, forested areas, and sandy dunes and beaches that form the coast characterize the land above water. These are divided by an intricate system of interconnecting waterways. Tidal waves sweep the area occasionally and, coupled with tidal movements and erosion that affect the area, cause much of the land to be constantly changing and reforming.

A variety of rare and endangered animals, including the Bengal tiger, live in the Sundarbans, a protected area that has been a national park since 1984 and on the World Heritage List since 1985.

KAPTAI LAKE

Kaptai Lake is one of the world's largest man-made lakes, covering about 300 square miles (777 square km). During the rainy season the lake can swell to about 400 square miles (1,036 square km). The lake was constructed during the building of the Karnaphuli hydroelectric plant in the late 1950s and early 1960s.

Situated roughly in the center of the Chittagong Hills, the dam displaced over 100,000 tribal people who lost their livelihood when much of the area's arable land was flooded. The Karnaphuli hydroelectric plant, however, remains an important source of power for Bangladesh today.

Kaptai Lake has been developed into a leisure destination, where people can rent resthouses and enjoy water sports.

THE BENGALI SEASONAL CYCLE

The Bengali year has six "seasons" of two months each that are related to the growing of cash crops. The new year begins on April 14 in the month of *Boishakh* ("bow-ee-SHAKH").

• The months of *Boishakh* and *Joishtho* ("JOSH-toh") are the season of *Grishsho* ("GRISH-show"), a warm summer period when rice and jute are cultivated.

• During *Borsha* ("BOR-shah"), the months of *Ashar* ("AH-shar") and *Shrabon* ("SRA-bon"), it rains incessantly and crops are harvested.

• *Sharad* ("shah-RUHD") marks the end of the monsoon rains in the months of *Bhadro* ("BAH-drow") and *Ashshin* ("AH-sheen"). Jute is collected and processed at this time.

• *Hemonto* ("HEH-mon-tow"), the months of *Kartik* ("KAR-tik") and *Ogrohayon* ("oh-gro-HOY-on"), begins a period of cooler weather when vegetable crops are planted.

• *Sheet* ("sheet") is the coolest season of the year. During the two months of *Sheet—Poush* ("po-SH") and *Magh* ("MAHG")—fresh fruit and vegetables are abundant.

• *Falgoon* ("fahl-GOON") and *Choitro* ("CHOY-trow") are the last two months of the year. This is the season of *Boshonto* ("boh-SHON-tow"), when the last of the *Sheet* crops are harvested and flowers blossom.

In early 1998 Bangladesh's worst cold snap in years left almost a hundred people, mostly the aged and homeless, dead. Temperatures dropped to 43°F (6°C) in the northern parts of the country and heavy fog disrupted bus, ferry, and airplane services.

Cyclones strike Bangladesh regularly, often with disastrous effects. The world's worst recorded cyclone in November 1970 killed some 500,000 people in Bangladesh.

CLIMATE

Bangladesh has a tropical monsoon climate. The year is divided roughly into three seasons: a hot, humid "build-up" from March to June, a rainy period from June to October, and a cooler, dry season from October to March. About 6% of the total land area is permanently flooded, but when the heavy monsoon rains fall, up to two-thirds of the land is deluged.

During the dry season, the land is parched and barren, and drought and consequently famine are major concerns. Farmers anxiously await the first monsoon rains, although coupled with this anticipation is a fear that the rains will be unsatisfactory. If the rains are too light they will be ineffective. If they are too heavy they could destroy the crops. The average annual rainfall varies between 55 inches (140 cm) in the dry Rajshahi area to over 197 inches (500 cm) in the Sylhet region.

FLORA AND FAUNA

Bangladesh enjoys a rich and varied flora and fauna. Tropical fruit such as mango, banana, papaya, coconut, and jackfruit grow abundantly throughout the country. The Chittagong Hills and the Sundarbans are covered with thick forests that yield valuable timber, some of which is processed to make newsprint.

Animal life is similarly abundant. Bangladesh has nearly 200 species of mammals, 750 species of birds, 150 species of reptiles, and over 200 species of marine and freshwater fish. The country's most famous animal is the Bengal tiger. Elephants, as well as several species of deer, including the barking deer, sambar, and spotted deer, live in the forests of the Chittagong Hills. Also found in Bangladesh are animals such as turtles, monkeys, gibbons, crocodiles, lizards, and snakes.

The jackfruit is popular not only in Bangladesh, but throughout southeast Asia.

Scientists believe stripes help tigers hide from their prey. Like human fingerprints, a tiger's stripes are unique—no two tigers have the same pattern of stripes.

THE BENGAL TIGER

The Bengal tiger is so important to the people of Bangladesh that Bangladesh is often referred to as "The Land of the Bengal Tiger," and the tiger is recognized as a national symbol.

The tigers predominantly live in the tropical jungles of the Sundarbans in the southwest of Bangladesh, but may also be found in parts of Nepal, India, Bhutan, and Burma. Growing up to 10 feet (3 m) in length and weighing up to 500 pounds (225 kg), the Bengal tiger eats medium to large prey such as pigs and deer. They have also been known to attack humans from time to time.

The tigers usually live for about 15 years in the wild; they live slightly longer in a controlled environment such as a zoo. These majestic animals were once populous, but because their pelts are highly prized and the people of some cultures believe that the bones have medicinal value, the Bengal tigers have themselves become prey and now number less than 5,000 in the wild. Another 300 live in zoos around the world.

Besides the Bengal tiger, other surviving subspecies of tigers include the Indochinese tiger, the Siberian tiger, the South China tiger, and the Sumatran tiger. Of these, the South China tiger is the most critically-endangered, with less than 30 living in the wild.

MAJOR CITIES

DHAKA Formerly known as Dacca, Dhaka is the capital of Bangladesh and its largest city. It is located almost exactly in the country's geographic center, in the region of the Ganges and Brahmaputra river deltas, and has a population of over four million, spread over approximately 117 square miles (303 square km).

Founded in the 10th century, Dhaka has since seen many changes. Under the Moghul empire, it was the capital of Bengal province from 1608 to 1704. Dhaka then became a trading center for British, French, and Dutch interests before it came under British rule in 1765. In 1905 it was made the capital of Bengal, and then became the capital of East Pakistan in 1956. The city suffered widespread damage during the 1971 war for independence. When Bangladesh won its independence from Pakistan, the name of the city was changed from the romanized version, Dacca, to the Bengali name of Dhaka.

Dhaka's railway station is one of the city's most striking modern buildings.

Dhaka is divided into an Old City and a New City, as well as residential and industrial areas. The Old City, which was developed when Dhaka was a center for Moghul trade, lies on the northern bank of the waterfront. Numerous historic sites dot the city, including Lalbagh Fort, an unfinished complex of buildings dating from 1678, and mosques and buildings from as far back as the 15th century.

The New City, which lies north of the Old City, is the business district and the commercial center of the city. Planning for the New City began in 1905, with tree-lined avenues and a large central lawn. The University of Dacca was founded here in 1921, but it was only after 1947 that rapid growth began to take place.

Built mostly on relatively firm, high ground, Dhaka enjoys easy access to the north by railways and roads and to the south by the many rivers.

CHITTAGONG The second largest city and the chief port of Bangladesh, Chittagong is about 12 miles (19 km) up the Karnaphuli River from the Bay of Bengal. About two million people live there. Chittagong is surrounded by hills, making it one of Bangladesh's most scenic cities. It is the commercial and manufacturing center of Bangladesh, and has extensively developed facilities for ocean liners.

KHULNA Khulna is primarily an industrial city, being home to Bangladesh's shipbuilding, telephone and cable, and newsprint industries. Khulna also has a university, a medical college, and a naval base. Sited along the Rupsa River, it is Bangladesh's third largest city, with a population of nearly a million.

Chittagong is an ancient city that has passed through phases of Buddhist, Hindu, and Muslim dominance. It came under Portuguese influence during the 16th century, before the city came under British control in 1760.

HISTORY

BANGLADESH IS A NEW NATION in a political sense, having been created in its present form less than 30 years ago in the aftermath of the 1971 war for independence. Its culture and civilization, however, go much further back in history, spanning over 3,000 years.

EARLY CIVILIZATION

An Austro-Asian race of people were the first inhabitants of the region in prehistoric times. Then came settlement by the Dravidians, Aryans, and Mongolians.

The earliest references to areas in Bangladesh can be found in the ancient texts of the *Ramayana* and the *Mahabharata*. These references are, however, mythological rather than historical. Reliable accounts became available only early in the fourth century B.C. It was around this

Opposite: **The spirit of the Bengali warrior is immortalized in these statues.**

Left: **The Martyrs' Memorial commemorates the thousands who died in the 1971 war for independence.**

time that the historians of Alexander the Great recorded accounts of a powerful civilization inhabiting the lower Ganges region, the Gandaridai. According to one of these historians, Diodorus, Alexander supposedly decided not to undertake an expedition against the Gandaridai after being "deterred by the multitude of their elephants." Greek geographer Ptolemy, who lived in the second century A.D., also made references in his works that can be traced to modern-day Bangladesh.

From the fourth century to the second century B.C., the region was dominated by the Mauryan empire, of which Asoka was the last major emperor. Little is known about the next few centuries until the rise of the Gupta empire in the fourth century A.D. The Guptas ruled the region until the dynasty's collapse in the seventh century and the rise of the first independent king of Bengal, Sasanka (ruled 603–663). The Gupta period was notable for its artistic development, much of which originated in the Bengal region. Gupta art later influenced the people of Southeast Asia.

ASOKA

Asoka reigned from 265 B.C. to 238 B.C. and was one of the greatest and noblest rulers the Indian subcontinent has known. It was his patronage of Buddhism that enabled the then fledgling religion to spread throughout India and eventually to east Asia.

His conquest of Kalinga on India's east coast in 261 B.C. marked a turning point in his life. Sickened by the death and suffering he caused, it was the last war he ever fought. Asoka embraced Buddhism and put the humane and benevolent ideals of Buddhism into practice, including the appointment of "Officers of Righteousness" who saw that the local authorities promoted "welfare and happiness" among his subjects. His famous edicts carved on rocks, in caves, and on specially erected pillars still survive today.

Renowned Chinese pilgrim Hsien Tsang, who visited the Bengal region between 639 and 645, wrote of the flourishing Buddhist states he found there. The Bengali language also began to assume a distinct form in the seventh century.

In the eighth century, following a century of chaos in Bengal, a warrior named Gopala was elected to the throne in an attempt to impose some semblance of order. Gopala reigned from 750 to 770 and began a dynasty that remained in power for over four centuries. The Pala dynasty he founded brought a long period of prosperity and stable government to the region. Its patronage nurtured the arts and sheltered the remnants of the Buddhists in the Indian subcontinent where Hinduism was becoming a powerful force. The Palas were thus the last powerful Buddhist monarchs on the subcontinent. They also established diplomatic relations with the kingdom of Srivijaya, which controlled much of the Indonesian archipelago.

The Palas were succeeded by the Sena dynasty during which Hinduism supplanted Buddhism. The Senas did not reign for long, however, as a more powerful force soon appeared.

One of the surviving mosques of Lalbagh Fort in Dhaka's Old City. Muhammad Azam, third son of Moghul emperor Aurangzeb, began the construction of the fort in 1678, but work was never completed.

ARRIVAL OF ISLAM

In the 13th century Muslim invaders from central Asia overthrew the Sena dynasty and converted most of the population to Islam. Thus began the Turkic domination of the region. Waves of Turks, Arabs, Pakhtuns, Persians, and other Muslims began migrating to Bengal, and a period of vigorous architectural achievement took place.

In 1556 Akbar acceded to the throne of the Moghul empire and began enlarging its borders. By 1576 Bengal had become a province within the empire. European traders—first the Portuguese, later the Dutch and British—began arriving. By 1616 the Portuguese had established a post in Dhaka. The decline of the Moghul empire began after the death of its last great emperor, Aurangzeb, in 1707. In the chaos that followed, British traders began to take over the region and the Indian subcontinent.

EARLY INDEPENDENCE MOVEMENTS

It is the events leading up to and during the 20th century that have resulted in the establishment of the nation of Bangladesh. British colonialists continually tried to strengthen their administrative control of east India, absorbing lands east of Calcutta, including the remaining portion of Bengal and the Ganges River valley. By 1859 the British had dominion of India from the Indus River in the west to Bengal in the east.

Under Lord Curzon, Bengal was divided into two separate provinces, West and East Bengal, in 1905. The partition provoked vociferous protests among the population that eventually led to the reunification of Bengal. The Muslim and Hindu factions of India, weary of being subordinate to the British, began to press for greater independence from the British government.

Lord Curzon (left), viceroy of India from 1898 to 1905, partitioned Bengal in 1905. Curzon was the youngest viceroy in the history of India.

The Hindu Indian National Congress primarily led the movement for independence. The Muslim faction became concerned about Hindu domination, and in 1906 they formed the All-India Muslim League. The League aimed to ensure proper consideration of Muslim needs. The Congress and the League coordinated their efforts in 1913, with the same fundamental goal in mind—self-government for India within the British empire. The Muslims were not satisfied, however, that their religious, economic, and political needs were being adequately protected. The next two decades were fraught with bitter conflicts between the Hindu and Muslim communities.

BANGLADESH AS PAKISTAN

In the 1930s the idea of a separate Muslim state arose as the solution to the conflicts. This state, eventually named Pakistan, was to be specifically dedicated to the religious ideals of Islam. Finally, after several years of debate, in 1947 India was given independence and Pakistan was created. Bengal was divided into East Bengal and West Bengal. West Bengal became part of the new Indian nation, while East Bengal was aligned with Pakistan.

It appeared that the quest for autonomy was over for the Bengali Muslims. However, almost from the moment Pakistan was formed, conflicts arose between the East and the West sectors of Pakistan. The first major difficulty was over the issue of language. The structure of Pakistan had left its political center, and thus its ruling elite, in the West, while the majority of the population lived in the East.

The last viceroy of India, Lord Louis Mountbatten, administered the transfer of power from Britain to the newly independent nations of India and Pakistan. He was assassinated in 1979 by Irish terrorists.

Mohammad Ali Jinnah, one of the Muslim leaders who led the move to form Pakistan, declared in a speech in 1948 that Urdu must become the official language of Pakistan. Curiously, Urdu was not the native tongue of any of the people of Pakistan, although some people could understand it reasonably well. Only little over 3% of the population spoke Urdu, as opposed to over 56% who spoke Bengali.

This seemingly illogical choice of Urdu as the national language was explained by suggesting that Urdu had a closer affinity to Arabic and Persian. Since Pakistan existed to accommodate Muslims, who derived their historical traditions from Moghul rule, Urdu was considered to be the appropriate choice of language. Urdu was coincidentally the language that was spoken by most of the politicians and was regarded as the elite language of Pakistan.

There was a strong feeling, particularly in East Pakistan, that the politicians were not satisfactorily representing all of Pakistan but were only protecting their personal interests. Considering Pakistan's unique geopolitical and socioeconomic structures, its diversity in culture, and the enormous geographic distance between the East and West, it was imperative to its survival that democratic power be given to both parts of the country on an equitable basis. The obvious neglect and exploitation of most of Pakistan by an elite class caused a division between the East and West, giving little chance for any national unity.

Mohammad Ali Jinnah (1876–1948), the first head of state of Pakistan. The four years he spent in England, studying law, sparked his interest in politics.

President Yahya Khan's actions in 1971 sparked off the war for independence.

WAR OF INDEPENDENCE

The Awami League, a Dhaka-based nationalist party, won the national elections in 1971, taking 167 of the 169 seats allotted to East Pakistan. This left the Awami League with an overall majority in the 313-member Pakistan National Assembly.

The president of Pakistan, Yahya Khan, dissatisfied with the results, postponed the opening of the National Assembly. Riots and strikes broke out in East Pakistan. Sheikh Mujibur Rahman, leader of the Awami League, then proclaimed the independence of Bangladesh on March 26, 1971.

Civil war immediately erupted, and Sheikh Mujibur Rahman was arrested and taken to West Pakistan. By April 1971 Pakistani soldiers had occupied all major towns. Resistance, however, continued. In November a major offensive by Mukhti Bahini (Liberation Army of East Bengal) guerrillas forced some 10 million people to flee into neighboring India. India subsequently declared war on Pakistan on December 4, joining the conflict. The combined forces of the Indian army, local guerrillas, and the civilian population eventually forced Pakistan's surrender on December 16, 1971.

In January 1972, Bangladesh was officially declared an independent nation. Sheikh Mujibur Rahman, who had been released by Pakistan's new president, Zulfikar Ali Bhutto, became the country's first prime minister.

A NEW NATION

The early years of Bangladesh's independence saw famine, martial law, military coups, and political assassinations. Floods in 1974 devastated the fragile Bangladeshi economy and led to famine and a cholera epidemic that left thousands dead. Sheikh Mujibur Rahman, who had banned all political parties except the Awami League and become the country's president, was assassinated in August 1975.

In the coups and counter-coups that followed, Chief of Army Staff General Ziaur Rahman took power. Political parties were legalized again, and in 1978 the extremely popular Zia won Bangladesh's first direct presidential election. Parliamentary elections followed in 1979, with Zia's Bangladesh Nationalist Party winning 49% of the total votes and 207 seats in the 300-seat parliament. Martial law was lifted and the state of emergency revoked. Zia went on to forge relationships with the West and the Islamic countries of the Middle East. In 1981, however, he was assassinated, and the government returned to a military dictatorship.

General Mohammad Ershad later seized power in a bloodless coup in March 1982 and placed the country under martial law. He became the prime minister and in December 1983 declared himself president. Although he won the presidential election in 1986, which was boycotted by both the Awami League and the Bangladesh Nationalist Party, there was growing opposition to his rule.

General Mohammad Ershad ruled Bangladesh from 1982 to 1990. He joined the army in 1953 and became chief of army staff in 1978 before seizing power in 1982.

In 1990 General Ershad was finally forced to resign by opposition groups and democracy was reestablished. Following elections in February 1991, General Zia's widow, Begum Khaleda Zia, was named prime minister.

After a time general dissatisfaction with the government grew and when she was reelected in 1996, voters questioned the legitimacy and integrity of the ballot. Once again, Bangladeshis went on strike and rallied against the reelected government. Begum Khaleda Zia eventually resigned. Fresh elections were held in June 1996 and a coalition government, headed by the daughter of Sheikh Mujibur Rahman, Sheikh Hasina Wajed of the Awami League, was elected.

Disgruntled Bangladeshis held a torchlight procession in support of a strike in 1992.

JUMMA HISTORY

The area of the Chittagong Hill Tracts was first colonized by the British in 1860, marking the first time in their history that the local tribes belonged to a state. The annexation was primarily a military strategy to enable the British to station troops on the eastern borders to defend themselves from intruders.

The next few years were a period of growing legal and commercial "Bengalization," with many Bengali businessmen converging on the region. As a result, the British government proclaimed itself the protector of tribal rights and implemented an exclusion policy that forbade Bengalis from dealing with the tribespeople in business or political matters. This policy worked, slowing down the process of Bengalization. But it also effectively isolated the Hill Tracts from the rest of Bengal and made the tribespeople dependent on the British.

The colonizers claimed ownership of the land and distributed prime portions to European entrepreneurs. They encouraged outsiders (other than Bengalis) to settle in the hills, forcing the tribespeople to relocate. The policy of exclusion had effectively deprived the Hill Tracts people of economic or political power, and consequently they took no part in decisions that directly affected them. Growing population pressure, overcultivation of the land, and the lack of nonagricultural employment eventually plunged the hill people into an economic crisis.

The hill tribes endured this situation until the 1970s, when Bangladesh was formed. The war for independence left Bangladesh overpopulated and in chronic poverty, and the idea to settle in the "empty" and "unutilized" Hill Tracts surfaced. The hill people were also regarded as less cultured, and it was felt that the Bengali migrants would help "civilize" them in the Bengali tradition. Not surprisingly, the hill people did not respond well to what they perceived as an invasion of their lands. They united as one group, calling themselves the Jummas, and retaliated with open rebellion.

The Bangladeshi government sent in the army and full-scale guerrilla warfare ensued. The conflict caused thousands of deaths and precipitated a mass exodus to refugee camps in India and Burma. However, in June 1997, peace talks between the leaders of the guerrilla movement and the new Bangladeshi government resulted in a consensus to end the conflict. The tension in the hills have not entirely eased, but the prospect of reconciliation provides hope for a peaceful future.

GOVERNMENT

THE PEOPLE'S REPUBLIC OF BANGLADESH HAS SEEN MANY CHANGES to its government since it was first established. The progression toward the form of government that exists today has been fraught with numerous political assassinations, martial law, and instances of corruption.

The constitution drawn up in 1972 created a parliamentary government, and promoted nationalism, secularism, socialism, and democracy as its basic principles. In 1975 this form of government was replaced by a presidential one in which the president held near-dictatorial power.

A coup d'état in 1981 marked the beginning of a 10-year military regime. In 1991 this dictatorship was overthrown and the government returned to the parliamentary system, with the election victory of Begum Khaleda Zia's Bangladesh Nationalist Party.

Above: **Sheikh Mujibur Rahman (1920–75), Bangladesh's first prime minister.**

Opposite: **Bangladeshis cast their votes. The voting age is 18.**

THE FIRST LEADER

Sheikh Mujibur Rahman, a founder-member of the Awami League, was the first prime minister of the independent sovereign nation of Bangladesh. He was named president at the first proclamation of Bangladeshi independence, but for almost the entire duration of the war, Mujib, as he was called, was imprisoned in West Pakistan.

He was charged and convicted of treason and sentenced to death. Upon the surrender of the Pakistani forces he was released and allowed to return to Bangladesh, where he assumed the presidency. Only two days later, he vacated that office to become prime minister.

Sheikh Mujibur Rahman arrives in Dhaka to a tumultuous welcome after his release from Pakistan in 1972.

Mujib pushed through a new constitution in which the nation would be led by a prime minister who would be appointed by the president and approved by a unicameral parliament. Over the first years of his leadership, Mujib did little to improve the country's social and economic problems. Nevertheless, he was reelected at the first national elections in 1973. His popularity decreased considerably after that as flooding, famine, and rising crime made it apparent that Mujib could not effectively resolve the country's problems.

In 1975 Mujib altered the constitution to make himself president for five years, giving him full executive powers. He then proclaimed Bangladesh a one-party state, effectively discarding the parliament and establishing himself as a dictator. Later that same year, Mujib, his wife, and three sons were assassinated by a group of young army officers.

STRUCTURE OF GOVERNMENT

Bangladesh has a republican government. The head of state is the president, who is elected by popular vote. The head of government is the prime minister, who leads a cabinet of ministers. These ministerial positions were formerly filled by presidential appointments, but now all positions are only given to candidates elected by popular vote.

The legislative assembly, called the House of the People, is a unicameral (single house) parliament with 300 seats. Legislative bills are passed by a majority vote of the members of parliament. A bill that has been passed by parliament goes to the president for approval. If the president gives his approval it becomes law. If not, it is returned to parliament for further debate. If it is passed a second time it will become law, regardless of presidential approval.

The president is elected for a term of five years and is eligible for re-election. The current president, Shahabuddin Ahmed, was elected in 1996.

Bangladesh's new parliament building in Dhaka. In addition to the 300 members of parliament who are elected by voters, another 30 women members are elected by the 300 members.

Sheikh Hasina Wajed, the current prime minister of Bangladesh, heads a council of ministers that includes several retired army officers.

THE PRIME MINISTER

The current prime minister, Sheikh Hasina Wajed, has been involved in Bangladeshi politics throughout her life. She was born the eldest daughter of Bangladesh's first prime minister, Sheikh Mujibur Rahman, who influenced her to join student politics during her college years.

She participated actively in events leading to the war for independence, which led to her imprisonment by the Pakistani army. When her father, mother, and three brothers were murdered in 1975 in an attempt to wipe out Mujibur's family, Wajed was visiting West Germany and so escaped death. For six years following her family's assassination, she remained in exile.

Since her return to Bangladesh in 1981, Wajed has worked steadily toward a democratic and fair government for the country, pressing for the resignation of two allegedly corrupt leaders and proposing the appointment of a nonpartisan caretaker government to conduct the national elections in June 1996.

In those elections Wajed led the Awami League to victory, winning 146 of the 300 contested seats. Her chief rival, the Bangladesh Nationalist Party, led by Begum Khaleda Zia, managed to win only 116 seats. By forging an alliance with the Jatiya Dal (National Party), which won 32 seats, and the Jatiya Samajtantrik Dal-Rab (National Socialist Party), which captured one seat, Wajed was able to form the government and was finally sworn in as the 10th prime minister of Bangladesh.

A LONG TIME TO WAIT

After years of unfulfilled promises that elections would be held "soon," Bangladesh finally held a general election in 1996—only the second free election in 25 years of self-government. Voters all over the country walked, bicycled, or rowed boats to the polls and waited in long lines for the opportunity to cast their votes. On the ballots, parties and candidates were represented by symbols to help the large proportion of illiterate voters.

Even this election, which was generally regarded as being free and fair, was difficult. At least 20 people were killed during the month-long campaign preceding it. Some 40,000 soldiers and 400,000 police and security forces were called in to reinstate order among the rival political activist groups. On election day itself, two more people were killed in gun battles outside two different polling stations.

"We want to form the government after the elections on the basis of national consensus. We want to build a society free from terrorism, corruption, and poverty. We want to fully equip the nation with the ability to enter the 21st century along with other developed countries of the world."

—Sheikh Hasina Wajed, campaign speech, May 10, 1996

MILITARY

The three arms of the Bangladeshi defense force—the army, navy, and airforce—were established in 1972, soon after the war for independence. Originally, all defense forces consisted mostly of deserters from the Pakistani forces, and most of their weapons and equipment were stolen or captured, or were spoils of the war.

The army now has around 100,000 troops; the navy, about 9,000; and the airforce, around 6,000. Service in the defense forces is voluntary and is not restricted by religious or ethnic affiliation. All male citizens over the age of 17 are eligible to join. Bangladesh's military equipment includes Russian- and Chinese-built tanks.

Bangladesh also has a paramilitary force of about 50,000, including some 30,000 border guards, the "Bangladesh Rifles."

POLICE

The Bangladeshi police force has been essentially rebuilt since 1972. The war for independence rendered the

SHANTI BAHINI

The Shanti Bahini (Peace Army) is a guerrilla army based in the Chittagong Hills. It was established in 1973 as the armed wing of the PCJSS, a political front of the people of the Chittagong Hill Tracts. Members of the Shanti Bahini have been fighting with the Bangladeshi government for more than 20 years. They seek recognition of the rights of the tribal communities in the region.

police system of East Pakistan completely ineffective, with most of its members defecting to join the Mukhti Bahini (the Liberation Army) or simply deserting.

At the top of the police hierarchy is the armed police. They are a highly-trained, elite unit, responsible for quelling violence and public disorder that is beyond the strength of the local police force. The armed police also operates an intelligence wing.

The general police force is administered by the inspector general. There are superintendents at district level and inspectors at subdistrict level. The local constabulary are the lowest rank in the police force. Although in general poorly-trained and poorly-equipped, the constabulary is integral to domestic security.

JUDICIARY

Government courts operate at regional, district, and subdistrict levels. Judges in these courts are appointed by the government. In addition, at the village level there is a form of magistrate court where disputes are initially taken.

These village courts are presided over by the local leader and two other judges, who are nominated by the disputing parties. Most cases are resolved in the village court, but in cases where one of the disputing parties desires another opinion, the case is taken to a government court of a higher level, and if taken far enough, eventually reaches the Supreme Court. The Supreme Court consists of a chief justice and other judges who are appointed by the president.

Above: **The Supreme Court in Dhaka.**

Opposite: A traffic policeman in Sylhet.

ECONOMY

DESPITE NATIONAL AND INTERNATIONAL EFFORTS to improve Bangladesh's economic situation, the country remains one of the world's poorest nations. The government has developed policies to reduce regulation of private industry, curb population growth, and expand employment opportunities through industrialization. However, these policies have only been partially successful in raising the Bangladeshis' standard of living.

The economy remains overwhelmingly dependent on agriculture. The frequent cyclones and floods that ravage Bangladesh and a rapidly growing workforce that cannot be absorbed into agriculture impede economic growth. Nonetheless some excellent rice harvests and the expansion of the garment export industry have contributed to modest growth, averaging some 4% in the 1990s.

Opposite: **A matchbox maker at work.**

Left: **A female shop- keeper in Bangladesh— a rare sight in a business overwhelmingly domi- nated by men.**

A rice farmer in southern Bangladesh.

THE WORKFORCE

In rural communities the work of women and men is strictly segregated, with men working in the fields and women doing the household chores. This is not the case in the cities. A large proportion of urban men work as rickshaw drivers or laborers, with the better-educated holding professional jobs.

Many women work as housemaids. As a rule, women do not work as waitresses or sales clerks. Nevertheless, it is now becoming more common to see well-educated women working as teachers, doctors, architects, and in other well-paid professions, though they are still comparatively few.

AGRICULTURE

Agriculture is by far Bangladesh's most important economic sector. It accounts for about 30% of the country's GDP and provides employment to two-thirds of the working population. Some 22.5 million acres (9.1 million hectares) of land are under cultivation.

Most farms in Bangladesh are small; a quarter of the estimated seven million farms are only one acre (0.4 hectares) or less. Another half are between one and four acres (0.4 and 1.6 hectares). Most of the small farms are cultivated by the owners and their families and provide a subsistence living. The larger farms benefit from the use of technology and fertilizers and produce a surplus that is sold in the markets. Their owners manage the farms and are considered the elite of rural society.

JUTE

Jute, *corchorus olitorius*, grows up to 4 feet (1.2 m) and bears shiny green leaves and bright yellow flowers that form elongated seedpods. Jute is second only to cotton as the world's most productive and useful fiber. The plant has been grown in Bangladesh since ancient times, but exports of raw jute to the West began only in the 1790s. Jute can be made into garments, carpets, twine, footwear, paper, and ornaments. Its single largest use, however, is in sacks and burlap bags that are used to ship grain, flour, sugar, and other agricultural produce. The leaves also make a tasty addition to cooking.

Bangladesh is the world's leading producer of jute and jute products, and jute production plays a dominant role in the country's economy. There are over 100 jute mills, jute textile mills, jute carpet mills, and jute twine mills, providing employment for thousands of Bangladeshis and bringing in a large proportion of national revenue.

Besides Bangladesh and India, jute is also grown in China and Brazil. Japan, Germany, and the United Kingdom are the world's largest importers of raw jute fiber.

The fibers of the jute plant are held together by a gummy material. Before the fibers can be extracted and used, the gum must be softened and removed. This is usually done by submerging bundles of harvested jute stems in a pool of water for up to a month to allow bacteria to break down the gummy tissues.

Drying rice in Cox's Bazar. Bangladesh is one of the great rice-growing countries of the world.

Bangladesh's major agricultural products are rice, jute, wheat, tea, sugarcane, cotton, tobacco, oilseeds, potatoes, beef, milk, and poultry. Jute and rice are the two most profitable crops.

Rice is harvested three times a year. The winter harvest in November/December is the most important and provides the best quality grain and the biggest crop. Winter-harvested rice is grown mainly in the lowlands, with the sowing done in May. The summer harvest in August/September is the next most important harvest and is grown on comparatively higher ground. Jute also grows well on the same land during the same period, so farmers must decide which crop to plant, depending on how well each did the previous season. If the prospects look better for jute, farmers may choose to plant more jute at the expense of rice. The third and smallest rice crop grows mainly in low-lying marshy areas.

A plantation worker picks tea leaves in Sylhet. The gentle slopes, rich light soil, and congenial climate of the Sylhet region are excellent for tea growing.

Tea plays a major role in the country's economy and is second only to jute as a money earner. The most important tea-growing regions are found in the east, in Sylhet and Chittagong. Thanks to improved production techniques and the use of better seeds, yields have increased dramatically over the last few decades.

Sugarcane has become an important cash crop, even though Bangladesh's climate and much of its land are not ideal for its cultivation. Rising domestic demand for sugar has ensured its continued popularity, despite the poor yields compared to other parts of the world.

Tobacco, another cash crop, is grown mainly in the north of the country. Rangpur is Bangladesh's leading tobacco-producing area. Its importance, however, has been declining as farmers favor other crops. Wheat, another minor crop, is grown mainly in the northern districts.

FISHING

Fish, a major part of the Bangladeshi diet, is also vital to the economy. The fish caught are mostly freshwater varieties, but overfishing has depleted stocks and ocean varieties are now increasingly common in the markets. The fishing industry is fairly unsophisticated in terms of technology, with many fishermen using hand-held nets.

Bangladesh also has several inland shrimp farms. The World Bank and the Asian Development Bank, as well as private investors, have financed projects to develop shrimp aquaculture by constructing new hatcheries and updating technology to increase the average yields.

More than a million tons (0.91 million metric tons) of fish are caught in Bangladesh every year.

MINERALS

Only a few mineral resources are commercially exploited in Bangladesh. The country has some reserves of natural gas, which is used for power generation and the production of nitrogenous fertilizer. All the gas is used domestically. The reserves are concentrated in the northeastern Sylhet region, as well as in several offshore reserves that remain untapped. It has been estimated that present reserves can support the country's needs until the year 2030.

Western Bangladesh has substantial coal deposits, but the lack of major prospective users in the area makes the exploitation of these deposits economically not viable. There are also unknown quantities of petroleum on land and offshore. In 1986 oil was discovered in the Haripur gas fields south of Sylhet. However, marketable quantities have yet to be found.

MANUFACTURING

Manufacturing employs about 12% of the workforce and contributes about 10% of the country's GDP. Mills making jute products lead the manufacturing industry today as a result of government industrial policies between 1947 and 1971 that gave priority to industries based on indigenous raw materials.

Newer ventures such as manufacturing ready-made garments contribute a significant share of the country's export earnings. Bangladesh also has factories producing leather products, fertilizers, sugar, newsprint, glass, aluminum, steel, and cement.

Oil drums in Chittagong. Most of Bangladesh's oil needs are met by imports.

Passengers hang precariously onto a van as it heads for Sylhet. Overloaded vehicles are a way of life for travelers in Bangladesh.

TRANSPORTATION

Bangladesh has a fairly extensive road system, with about 6,000 miles (9,700 km) of main roads and 4,200 miles (6,800 km) of paved secondary roads. There are three main crossings into Bangladesh from India—at Benopol-Haridispur, on the Calcutta route; at Chilihari-Haldibari, on the Darjeeling route; and at Tamabil-Dawki, on the Shillong route. Prior to the 1950s there were several overland routes between the subcontinent and Burma, but these were closed for political reasons.

The country has only about 40,000 privately-owned cars and 135,000 motorcycles. Buses provide a cheap mode of transport for Bangladeshis. In the cities rickshaws are the most common taxi service. In Dhaka alone, rickshaws provide employment for about a quarter of the workforce and transportation for about two-thirds of the population.

Trains are also popular. There are nearly 1,860 miles (3,000 km) of railway lines running through Bangladesh. Difficulties arise, however, when traveling by train between Dhaka and points west of the capital—unbridged rivers break rail journeys, the routes are circuitous, and the rail gauges between the east and the west of the country are different.

The most common mode of transport between towns, and indeed the distinguishing feature of Bangladesh's transportation system, is by water, on boats and ferries that operate along the numerous waterways. A paddle-wheel steamer runs between Dhaka and Khulna regularly, and many other ferries shuttle passengers from port to port.

Bangladesh has international airports at Dhaka, Chittagong, and Sylhet, as well as seven domestic airports. Bangladesh Biman Airlines is the state-owned airline.

Above: **A fully-laden ferry crosses Meghna River.**

Overleaf: **A souvenir vendor at Cox's Bazar, one of the country's top tourist attractions.**

TOURISM

Tourism is still a minor source of foreign exchange income for Bangladesh, although news reports of famine, floods, and political unrest have done little to improve foreign perception of Bangladesh.

However, increasing numbers of tourists are attracted to the country's sights and culture. Tourist attractions include historical sites in Dhaka and Chittagong, and the beaches of Cox's Bazar, the town founded in 1798 by Captain Hiram Cox of the East India Company.

The majority of visitors are from India, Pakistan, Japan, the United Kingdom, and the United States. Many travelers also use Bangladesh as a link to India, taking advantage of cheap flights from Europe.

TRADE

Bangladesh's chief exports include ready-made garments, jute, fish and shrimps, hides, skins, leather, and tea. Textile yarn and fabrics, machinery and transport equipment, petroleum, and chemicals are some of its major imports.

Its top trading partners include the United States, India, the United Kingdom, Japan, Hong Kong, China, and Singapore.

THE GRAMEEN BANK

Dr. Muhummad Yunus, a professor of economics from the University of Chittagong, first came up with the idea of the Grameen Bank in 1976. Yunus was concerned by the extraordinary poverty that surrounded him. Speaking to a poor village woman, he discovered that she earned merely a few cents a day weaving, most of which she had to give to the merchant who rented her a loom and to local moneylenders, who charged an outrageous 50% interest. Yunus heard many similar stories from villagers and he determined to find a way to help release these people from the debilitating poverty and debts that ruled their lives.

What transpired was a revolutionary banking system that promoted the following ideals: to provide banking facilities for the poor, to eliminate the exploitation of moneylenders, to create opportunities for self-employment for the underemployed and unemployed, to raise economic, social, and political awareness among its members, and most importantly, to provide an escape from the cycle of "low income, low savings, low investments, low income" to the cycle of "low income, investment, more income, more investment, more income."

The Grameen Bank's customers are the landless, most of whom have never dealt with a lending institution before. About 93% of the borrowers are women. People require loans for various activities, such as housing, business enterprises, and financial investments. The Grameen Bank provided 200,000 people with collateral-free loans in its first 10 years and had a 98% recovery rate of loans, despite many doubts that poor people, especially women, would be able to honor their debts. In place of the collateral required by conventional banks, small groups of about five people come together to create a morally-binding guarantee of repayment. Around 3,000 "bicycle bankers" are employed to work in the field, supervising the borrowers' finances.

The Grameen Bank has had astounding success in improving the economic condition of thousands of Bangladeshis. It has had a major impact on poverty alleviation, lifting 80% of its clients above the poverty line and providing the means for self-employment beyond agricultural labor.

BANGLADESHIS

BANGLADESH IS THE EIGHTH MOST POPULOUS COUNTRY IN THE WORLD, with a population almost half that of the United States living in an area slightly smaller than Wisconsin. It is also the most densely populated of all countries having an area of over 1,000 square miles (2,600 square km). Bangladesh's population density is 2,212 people per square mile (854 per square km).

Since gaining independence, Bangladesh has experienced massive population growth. In 1996 the country had an estimated population of 123 million and a growth rate of 2.3%. Bangladeshi women have a high fertility rate, averaging 4.4 children per woman. This, coupled with a comparatively low ratio of deaths (11 per 1,000) to births (31 per 1,000), means a fast increasing and young population. Almost half of Bangladesh's population is under 15 years.

Average life expectancy is low, at 55.5 years, compared to well over 70 years for developed countries such as the United States, Japan, and the United Kingdom. The individual averages for Bangladeshi men and women are almost similar, despite higher incidences of malnutrition and disease among women.

Above and opposite: **Bangladeshis, young and old, are proud of their rich heritage and language.**

SOCIAL CLASSES

The Bangladeshi class system is not, in general, rigidly stratified. The social classes are mostly functional and allow considerable mobility. Generally, classes are defined by wealth and power as opposed to hereditary social

The family unit provides the framework that makes up Bangladeshi society.

distinctions. In addition, Islam has fairly egalitarian principles that influence social structure.

The exception to this is the caste system traditionally observed by Hindus, but this has not featured very strongly in the Hindu communities of Bangladesh. About 75% of Bangladeshi Hindus belong to low caste and untouchable groups; only a small minority are of the middle or professional caste, and none are high caste. The professionals are therefore the highest caste of Hindus in Bangladesh. However, being Urdu-speakers, they became somewhat alienated in independent Bangladesh. In the social arena, the castes are increasingly able to interact with each other. While all Hindus will identify themselves with a particular caste, caste distinction has gradually come to play a less significant role than it traditionally played in Hindu society.

ATTITUDES

Bangladeshi attitudes are very much rooted in village traditions. Bangladesh is predominantly a country of rural people living simple country lives, and while modern ideas occasionally influence thinking, the attitudes of the people are dominated by traditional beliefs, customs, and manners.

DRESS

Bangladeshi men and women dress modestly. Women generally wear *saris* ("sa-REES"). The sari, a cloth several yards long, is of a width that stretches from waist to ankle. It is wound around the body from the waist,

A young Bangladeshi woman enjoys a day at the beach.

over an ankle-length slip, and its free end is thrown over one shoulder. Muslim women drape the free end around their head, and sometimes over the lower part of their face. Cotton *saris* are worn during the work day while silk ones are reserved for special occasions. Muslim women, in particular, favor bright colors and patterns and like to decorate their clothes with intricate embroidery. For a wedding, it is traditional for the bride to wear red and yellow.

Men wear *lungi* ("LOONG-gee"), a garment similar to the sarong worn by the Malays of Southeast Asia, that are wrapped around the waist. This is usually accompanied by a Western-style shirt. For formal occasions a man may wear an ankle-length, collarless jacket called a *sherwani* ("sher-WAH-nee"), a turban, and traditional decorative slippers called *nagra* ("NAH-grah").

Business people and professionals, especially the men, may don Western-style clothes of pants, shirt, and tie as they go about their work in the cities. It is, however, rare to find Bangladeshis wearing these elsewhere. Bangladeshi women are rarely seen wearing pants, short skirts, or revealing dresses in public—these are likely to incur society's strong disapproval.

ETHNIC MINORITIES

JUMMAS

Jumma is a generic term that refers to the people of 12 distinct tribes inhabiting the Chittagong Hill Tracts. With a population of less than a million people, Jummas constitute less than 1% of the total population of Bangladesh. They are of Sino-Tibetan descent and have distinct Mongoloid features. Essentially an agricultural people, they practice swidden cultivation, locally known as *jhum* ("juhm"), from which their name is derived. Their chosen style of agriculture makes Jummas relatively nomadic; they do not establish permanent homes, but move around constantly.

Opposite: **A young Bangladeshi girl in a brightly-colored** *sari.*

Left: **An inhabitant of the Chittagong Hill Tracts.**

SWIDDEN CULTIVATION

The swidden method of cultivation, also called slash-and-burn or shifting cultivation, is practiced by many cultures around the world. In this method the area that is farmed is rotated every few years, so that no area becomes overworked and damaged. At the start of each season, when a new field is needed, an area of several acres is slashed and burned, clearing the area of all vegetation. The ash that falls over the ground serves as a natural fertilizer on top of the thin forest soils. The earth is then prepared and sown by hand.

In the first couple of years the yield is bountiful. However, with exposure to the sun, the thick, moist loam on the forest floor begins to degenerate into barren sand and clay. At this point, the farmers will abandon the site and clear a new field. Because the land has not been allowed to degenerate too much, the natural forests soon reclaim the old field and restore the richness in the soil. That patch of land will not be cultivated again for many years, long enough at least for the natural vegetation to rejuvenate.

The tribes are essentially Buddhist, or practice a combination of Buddhism and tribal religion. Each tribe has a unique language, mostly deriving from the Tibeto-Burmese language family, and a unique system of social organization. In the past there was intertribal warfare, but in recent years the tribes have formed an alliance based on common land and history, as opposed to religion, language, or culture.

BIHARIS

The Biharis are Urdu-speaking non-Bengali Muslims originating from Bihar in northern India. They originally came to Bengal as refugees. Before independence, the Biharis were the dominant people of Bengali society; as such they did not stand to benefit from the separation from Pakistan.

During the war they chose to ally themselves with Pakistan. When independence was announced for Bangladesh, hundreds of thousands of Biharis were repatriated to Pakistan, leaving only 600,000 Biharis in Bangladesh.

AMAR SHONAR BENGAL (MY GOLDEN BENGAL)

Bangladesh's national anthem was composed by Rabindranath Tagore (1861–1941), who won the Nobel Prize in literature in 1913.

> My Bengal of gold, I love you
> Forever your skies, your air set my heart in tune
>   as if it were a flute,
> In Spring, Oh mother mine, the fragrance from
>   your mango-groves makes me wild with joy—
>   Ah what a thrill!
>
> In Autumn, Oh mother mine,
>   in the full-blossomed paddy fields,
> I have seen spread all over—sweet smiles!
> Ah, what beauty, what shades, what an affection
>   and what a tenderness!
> What a quilt have you spread at the feet of
>   banyan trees and along the banks of rivers!
> Oh mother mine, words from your lips are like
>   nectar to my ears!
>   Ah, what a thrill!
> If sadness, Oh mother mine, casts a gloom on your face,
>   my eyes are filled with tears!

Although born in Calcutta, India, Rabindranath Tagore is claimed by Bangladeshis as their most famous literary figure. Tagore spent 10 years in East Bengal (now Bangladesh), managing his family's estates. During this time he grew to love the countryside, and the Padma River became an often-repeated image in his verse. In the last years of his distinguished life, he took up painting and had his works exhibited in Europe and the United States.

Opposite: **A Bihari family awaits repatriation to Pakistan in 1972. Biharis now make up less than 1% of Bangladesh's population.**

LIFESTYLE

BANGLADESH IS ONE OF THE LEAST URBANIZED COUNTRIES in the world. An overwhelming proportion of its population live in the country, and village life, with agriculture providing work, is the typical lifestyle for most Bangladeshis.

Nevertheless, like the rest of the developing world, Bangladesh's cities have become beacons attracting those who seek a better life for themselves and their families. Young males form the majority who make the journey to the urban centers to find work in the new industries that accompany development. In manufacturing, for example, male workers outnumber female workers almost three to one.

The more adventurous seek work in the more dynamic economies of Asia, with many heading for the plantations, construction sites, and service industries of countries like Malaysia and Singapore.

In 1997, some 300,000 Bangladeshi workers in Malaysia, one of the most popular destinations for Bangladeshis, sent back about US$100 million to their home country.

Opposite: **Home for this couple is a makeshift shed among the slums in Khulna.**

Left: **A villager transports rice bags with the help of a pole.**

SOCIAL CONVENTIONS

GREETINGS Bangladeshis greet each other by saying "*Shagatom*" ("SHAH-gah-tom"), meaning "welcome." The standard greeting among Hindus is the *namaste* ("NAHM-ahst-ay"), where the head is bowed and the palms are placed together in front of the chest with fingers pointing upward, as if praying.

GENDER SEPARATION There is very strict gender separation within the Muslim community. In school, boys and girls are seated separately and are given different areas in which to play. Within the home, certain areas are designated specifically "male" or "female" areas. Women and men are segregated in the mosque when they go to pray, and there are certain places that women will rarely go, such as a bank.

NO OFFENSE INTENDED!

There are a number of body gestures that Westerners use at home that would be interpreted as grave insults by a Bangladeshi. The act of raising your thumb to someone, for example, is a friendly gesture of encouragement or approval in the United States. In Bangladesh, however, this is considered very rude.

It is acceptable for men to sit cross-legged and for women to sit with their legs tucked beneath them and to one side on the floor or cushions, but it is taboo to display the soles of your feet. It is also offensive to offer money as a gift.

Men and women are expected to dress and behave modestly. Flirting is completely unacceptable.

Bangladeshi men will shake the hand of a Western man, but when introduced to a woman he simply nods his head as it is taboo for a man to touch a woman who is not a family member.

Bangladesh's population is growing fast, with more than three million babies born every year.

BIRTH

Many Bangladeshi women, particularly in the rural areas, give birth at home rather than in a hospital. The women often go to their natal home, especially for their first child. A room in the house is designated for this purpose and is called the *atur ghar* ("ah-TOO ghor"), or birthing room, for 40 days after the birth. The baby is born in the presence of female relatives or friends. If a midwife is called in—rarely in the case of poor families—she will often only come to cut the umbilical cord. Poor women must deliver the baby themselves.

Childbirth is regarded as highly polluting, to both the mother and her surroundings. After childbirth, the mother and the newborn are confined to the birthing room for up to nine days, and allowed out only for natural functions. Even then, the mother must be accompanied by another woman, and must carry a sickle and a burning dung stick to protect her from evil spirits, to which she is believed to be vulnerable at that time.

A small fire burns constantly in the birthing room, filling it with smoke that is said to protect the mother and baby from harmful spirits. After her confinement is over the mother has a ritual bath, the birthing room is swept and plastered, and the bed linen is boiled to purify it. Forty days after the birth the mother and the birthing room are ritually cleansed again, and then the mother resumes her usual activities.

MARRIAGE

Marriages are usually arranged by the bride's father or another male guardian. Either the proposed bride or groom may refuse a match; however, this is rare, as it is a social disgrace to do so. Although girls traditionally marry at the onset of puberty, the average age has increased in recent years to around 18. There is usually a considerable age difference between the bride and the groom. Dowries are traditional and, despite laws prohibiting the practice, are still usually offered and accepted.

Above: **A lavish wedding of two young Bangladeshis from wealthy families in a Dhaka hotel.**

Overleaf (left): **Most girls in Bangladesh will marry while in their teens. A mature unmarried woman is considered an embarrassment to her family.**

Overleaf (right): **A man with his child.**

Wedding ceremonies vary depending on the religion of the bride and groom. Muslim-style weddings are most common, although most weddings incorporate cultural elements into the religious traditions. There are usually four parts to a Bangladeshi wedding: the *gae halud* ("gay ho-LUTH"), *akht* ("AHKT"), the *mala badol* ("MAY-lah BA-dol"), and the *bou bhat* ("boa BAHT").

The *gae halud* translates as the turmeric ceremony and originates from a Bengali tradition. One ceremony is held for the bride and another for the groom, with the bride's generally taking place first. Friends and family of the groom arrive with gifts of *saris*, jewelry, and cosmetics for the bride, and the bride's family gives them sweets and flower petals.

The bride sits on a dais decorated with flowers and the groom's mother ties a golden-fringed bracelet around her wrist as a symbol of betrothal. Well-wishers then approach the dais one by one to place a bit of turmeric on the bride's face and their own, and then feed the bride something sweet. The groom's ceremony is similar.

The *akht* ceremony, which is part of Islamic tradition, is the legal declaration of marriage. As in a Christian wedding, the bride and groom exchange vows. First the consent of the groom is obtained without the bride present, then the groom asks the bride if she consents. She accepts by saying *kobul* ("koh-BUL," I accept) three times. The couple then share the fruit of a date palm, an Islamic custom.

The *mala badol* is a ceremony in which the bride and groom exchange garlands, symbolizing their union. A muslin cloth is placed over the head of the couple and they share a spicy yogurt drink. Then they glance at each other through a mirror. Traditionally this glance was the first time that the couple would have seen each other.

Several days later, the groom's family hosts the *bou bhat* (bride's rice), which is a reception for the newlyweds. This is the first time that the couple steps out socially as husband and wife.

DEATH

It is Islamic custom to prepare the deceased by washing the body and wrapping it in a shroud. The body is then buried and the men pray.

Women do not participate in the burial or burial prayers nor visit graves because their presence is believed to contaminate the sacred ground.

Above: **A buffalo gets a wash from its owner.**

Opposite: **A village wife prepares the evening meal.**

RURAL LIFE

About 82% of Bangladeshis live in the country, reflecting the high proportion of agricultural workers. The rural Bangladeshi home, or *bari* ("BAH-ree"), typically consists of a collection of individual huts gathered around a central courtyard. The plot of land is usually rectangular, with the narrow end abutting the street. The different areas of a *bari* have specific purposes. On the street side of the house is a fairly large area called the *goli* ("GOH-lee"). This is a semiprivate space that is predominantly used by men for socializing and receiving male guests.

A BANGLADESHI HOUSEWARMING

When a new house is built, a traditional Bangladeshi buries a nail under each of its four corners in the belief that this secures it from falling down. Before moving in, Muslim families will call in a *mullah* ("mu-LAH," a learned man) to recite verses from the Koran. Wealthier families may hold a *milad* ("MI-lahd"), a religious gathering to pray and discuss the life of Prophet Mohammed.

The *ghar* are the individual one- or two-room huts. They are generally constructed with mud walls and thatched roofs, and often have no windows and only one doorway for light. They are used mostly for storage and sleeping, although work moves inside during wet weather. The *ghar* are focused around the courtyard, which is the most important part of the *bari*. This is where all the daily activities, socializing, and celebrations take place.

The courtyard is the women's area, and while nonrelated females may move freely through the courtyards of neighbors, it is kept private from unrelated males. For a man to enter the courtyard uninvited is perceived as a symbolic violation. The *kanta* ("KAN-tah") is the garden at the rear of the *bari*. It contains the vegetable patch, bamboo grove, and fruit trees, and often a private pond for bathing. There is also a handpump for drawing water. The *kanta* is also a woman's domain.

A *bari* is typically inhabited by an extended family, each nuclear family having its own *ghar*, but all sharing the other areas of the *bari*. Sons will build their own *ghar* when they marry, but will remain under their father's authority, and their wives under their mother-in-law's. When the father dies, sons will often start their own separate households.

A crowded market in the northeastern city of Sylhet.

URBAN LIFE

Approximately 18% of Bangladeshis live in an urban environment. Towns are populated mostly by government employees, merchants, and business operators. A majority of these people live in shabby, ramshackle constructions lacking modern amenities. Unlike rural homesteads, urban dwellings are usually shared by a nuclear family. Only occasionally does the extended family live together.

Dhaka and much of urban Bangladesh suffers from poverty and inadequate housing. A 1991 survey reported 2,156 slums in Dhaka, providing for a population of 718,143 people in 789 acres (320 hectares). That is a population density of 910 people per acre (2,244 per hectare), all inhabiting slums. The survey also found that:

• 81% of the slums had been established after Bangladesh gained independence;

• 62.7% of slum dwellers had no access to gas; and

• 36.1% of slum dwellers had no access to electricity.

WOMEN'S ROLES

Muslim countries are overwhelmingly male-dominated. Women have low social status and, as they are generally prevented from taking up income-earning work, are considered a financial burden on their family. From an early age boys and girls are treated differently. At school, girls and boys are segregated in the classroom, even in coeducational schools.

There is a strict division of labor according to gender: men are the income earners, women perform work in the household. A woman's duties include hand-grinding flour and spices, taking care of animals other than cattle (this being the man's job), tending the vegetable garden, pumping water, replastering and repairing the home when necessary, and processing and storing farm produce. Few women have wage-earning employment; those who do, earn wages of around 20–30% of the wages earned by men. Women who have jobs usually work in factories. Those with more education may work in government jobs, such as health care or teaching, but the numbers remain few.

In the villages, a labor-intensive task such as collecting water is solely a woman's responsibility.

71

A primary school student receives extra attention from her teacher. The country's ablest students can aspire to Bangladesh's largest university, the University of Dhaka. There are nine other universities in the country, including specialist universities for engineering and technology, agriculture, and Islamic studies.

EDUCATION

Poor education is a major contributing factor to Bangladesh's socio-economic problems. Despite moves since the 1970s to improve educational facilities, Bangladesh still does not have enough schools. Parents also lack incentives to send their children to school, when more pressing needs, such as food, must be met.

Although primary education is free in Bangladesh, attendance is low, with only 17 million students enrolled in about 96,000 primary schools. Bangladesh's 11,500 secondary schools have less than five million students. As a result, the country suffers from a low literacy rate of less than 40%. Illiteracy is particularly high among women because parents prefer to send boys to school, keeping girls at home to help with the household work. Often a religious education is all that is deemed necessary for girls. Most women can read the Koran and pray (both in Arabic) and have knowledge of Islamic history.

HEALTH

Bangladesh suffers from major health problems. Malnutrition and poor sanitation cause hundreds of deaths every year. Susceptibility to disease is high and availability of treatment low. While Bangladesh has a basic health care system in place, it is grossly inadequate.

The Bangladeshi government's objective is to provide minimum health care services for all. In 1996 about 20 million children were inoculated against polio as part of a campaign to eradicate the disease. Nevertheless financial constraints and the lack of supplies and personnel continue to inhibit the government's plans. With only about three beds per 10,000 people, Bangladesh ranks alongside Afghanistan, Ethiopia, and Nepal as countries with the world's lowest provision of hospital beds. In contrast Monaco has 168 hospital beds for every 10,000 people.

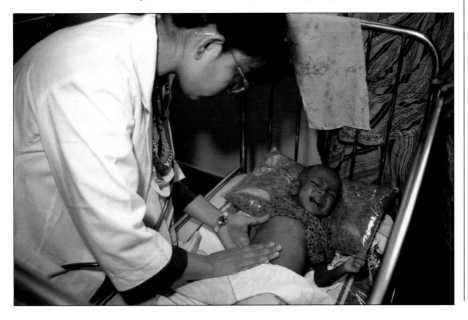

A doctor at work in a hospital nutrition unit in Dhaka. Bangladesh has 120,000 medical workers (doctors, nurses, and midwives), serving its population of 123 million.

RELIGION

BANGLADESH WAS CREATED AS A MUSLIM COUNTRY. Some 85% of its population ascribe to Islam, making it one of the largest concentrations of Muslims in the world. Hindus form another 12% of the population, while Buddhists, Christians, and followers of tribal religions make up the rest.

PRE-ISLAMIC RELIGIONS

Bangladesh's places of worship recall its Buddhist and Hindu heritage. There are still several Buddhist monasteries dating from the seventh to ninth centuries A.D., which are state-protected. Many other monasteries, however, were destroyed by invading Muslim armies in the 13th century, in the belief that they were military fortresses.

Opposite: **The Qassabtuly Jame Mosque in Dhaka.**

Left: **Bangladesh's oldest Koran—a handwritten copy several centuries old.**

75

THE STORY OF ISLAM

Islam came into existence in A.D. 610, when a man named Mohammed first preached a series of divine revelations to the people of the Arabian city of Mecca. His words were believed to have been told to him by the angel Gabriel and he was accepted by many as the Prophet of God. Mohammed was a firm monotheist (believer in one God). This made him unpopular with many Meccans, and in 622 he and the followers his preachings had attracted were driven from Mecca to Medina.

This migration marks the beginning of the Muslim calendar. Today Mecca is Islam's holiest city. It is every Muslim's goal to visit Mecca and the Kaaba ("KAH-AH-bah"), a building covered in black cloth that stands in the courtyard of the Great Mosque, the holiest place in Mecca.

Mohammed continued to preach, and after his death in 632 his divinely-inspired speeches were compiled into the Koran, the scripture of Islam. The Koran and the Hadith ("HAH-dith"), a collection of Mohammed's sayings and examples of his personal behavior, are now the comprehensive guide to spiritual, ethical, and social living for millions of Muslims all over the world.

THE FIVE PILLARS OF ISLAM

These are the duties of all Muslims:

SHAHADAH ("shah-HAH-dah") This is a testimonial prayer that states the central belief of Islam—there is no god but Allah, and Mohammed is his Prophet.

Opposite: **A Muslim performs one of his five daily prayers. A special functionary intones a call to prayer at the appropriate hours and people gather at the mosque.**

PURDAH

Muslim girls dress with modesty in mind. This prepares them for the restrictions of *purdah* ("PERH-dah") practices, a regulating code of behavior for women. A woman usually drapes the end of her *sari* over her head when in the presence of adult males. Outside her home she often clenches part of her *sari* with her teeth to obscure her face.

Worshipers gather at the Baitul Mukkaram Mosque, Dhaka's largest mosque.

SALAT ("sah-LAHT") This is a daily prayer recited five times: at sunrise, midday, afternoon, sunset, and evening.

ZAKAT ("zah-KAHT"), or almsgiving, requires that Muslims give money to the poor or to charitable causes.

SAWM ("soom") is the fast during Ramadan ("RUM-ah-dahn"), the ninth month of the Islamic year, when Muslims abstain from various activities, including eating and drinking, between the hours of sunrise and sunset.

HAJJ ("hahj") is the pilgrimage to Mecca. All Muslims should make the pilgrimage to the holy city at least once in their life if they can. Some perform the *hajj* many times. A male pilgrim wears a seamless white garment and abstains from sexual relations, shaving, and cutting the hair or nails. While in Mecca the pilgrim performs certain rituals that emulate actions of figures from Arabic history, such as running between the hills of Safa and Marwa in imitation of Hagar, the wife of Abraham, who was the father of the Arabs. A highlight of the *hajj* is the kissing of the sacred black stone of Islam housed in the Kaaba.

Islam has hundreds of millions of followers around the world. Some five million Muslims live in the United States alone. Indonesia, with some 85% of its 200 million people professing the religion of Islam, has the world's largest Muslim population.

PRAYER RITUAL

Praying is a very public event in Bangladesh. Whenever possible, men will congregate at a mosque. Women sometimes congregate separately from the men, but more often pray in their homes. The form of prayer is strictly prescribed by Islam. Everybody stands upright, facing toward Mecca, and then performs the following ritual, called *raka* ("RAH-kah"), which is repeated several times:

- Open the hands.
- Touch the earlobes with the thumbs.
- Lower the hands and fold them, right hand over left.
- Bow from the hips with hands on knees.
- Straighten the body.
- Sink gently to the knees.
- Touch the ground with hands, nose, and forehead, remaining 10–15 seconds in this position.
- Raise the body while kneeling, sitting on the heels.
- Count on the fingers.
- Press the hands, nose, and forehead to the ground again.
- Stand.

HINDUISM

Hindus first overthrew Buddhist rule in the region of Bangladesh in about A.D 1100, only a century before the Muslim invasion. Hinduism has been a minority religion there ever since. Most religious observances take place in the home, where there is usually a shrine or altar. When Hindus visit a temple, it is not generally a community gathering, as with Islamic prayers and Christian services. Instead they go alone or in small groups to pray and worship the gods. Cows are held sacred by Hindus and are never eaten. Although vegetarianism is common among high caste Hindus of other countries, most Bangladeshi Hindus of higher caste eat some fish.

Opposite: **A Buddhist monk in the Chittagong Hill Tracts. Buddhism was founded by Prince Gautama Siddhartha in the sixth century B.C.**

Right: **Hindu Bangladeshis. Freedom of worship is guaranteed by the country's constitution.**

BUDDHISM

Buddhism was the dominant religion in Bangladesh before the Muslim conquest. After the invading Muslim armies destroyed the monasteries and thus the centers of learning, Buddhism diminished rapidly.

Today, there are few Buddhists in Bangladesh. Most are concentrated in the Chittagong Hill Tracts, where there are still several monasteries. Most Buddhist villages have a school where boys live for a time and learn to read Burmese and scriptures in Pali. It is not uncommon for adult men to regularly return to their school for periods of retreat.

CHRISTIANITY

Members of the small Christian community of Bangladesh are mostly Roman Catholics. The first Christian settlements were established in Dhaka by the Portuguese in the 17th century. Later, Protestant and Baptist missions were also established. The church found a large number of converts, particularly among low-caste Hindus.

THE SPIRIT WORLD

Many Bangladeshis, particularly rural villagers, believe in an active spirit world that is largely associated with women. Consequently, a woman's movements are restricted because of the fear of spirit possession. A menstruating woman, for example, will not go near big trees or leave home after dark. Similarly a pregnant woman will not leave her home on full moon days or eclipses for fear of giving birth to a deformed child.

LANGUAGE

BENGALI, THE OFFICIAL LANGUAGE OF BANGLADESH, is the seventh most widely spoken language in the world, with over 180 million native speakers. There are also several hundred thousand speakers of Urdu in Bangladesh, and a number of languages similar to Burmese.

Bangladeshis are generally articulate and expressive, despite their low literacy rate. And more so than in most countries, language in Bangladesh has particular significance in the hearts and minds of its speakers. After having fought a long and gruesome war for the right to speak Bengali, the Bangladeshis now regard their language as a symbol of their nationalism.

DEVELOPMENT OF BENGALI

Bengali developed from the Aryan, or Indo-Iranian, branch of the Indo-European language family. It is derived from Prakrit (Middle Indo-Aryan),

Opposite: **Colorful signs on the rear of a taxi.**

Left: **Three young Bangladeshis practice writing. In Bangladesh girls are often withdrawn from school when they reach puberty.**

which was itself derived from Sanskrit. Bengali, or Bangla as it is also called in Bangladesh, was identifiable from about A.D. 1000. A collection of Buddhist texts found in Nepal, dated between 900 and 1,000 years old, are the oldest known written records of Bengali.

The written form has been subjected to remarkably little local variation. The records that exist reveal nearly identical forms of language from divergent civilizations. The spoken language, however, has been gradually conditioned by the various linguistic and ethnic influences in the different regions, and many new Indo-Aryan speech forms have emerged.

Bengali developed as a "people's" language and remains so today. One of the earliest records of Bengali is the Buddhist *Charyapad* ("CHAH-ree-AH-pad"), which was influenced by the ballads and experiences of Buddhist monks of north Bengal who worked among villagers. These writings were themselves influenced by the vernacular of the villagers, and so the language, from its earliest roots, has been a true expression of its speakers, not intellectualized.

FORMAL AND COLLOQUIAL STYLES

Two main styles of Bengali are used. *Sadhubhasa* ("SAH-DOO-bah-sah")
is the "elegant language." It is the traditional literary style based on the
Middle Bengali of the 16th century. *Chaltibhasa* ("CHAHL-tee-bah-sah"),
the "current language," only really developed during the 20th century. It
is based on the cultivated speech of the educated from around Calcutta.

The differences between the two styles are subtle. The vocabulary is
much the same, although there are differences in the forms of pronouns
and verbs. *Chaltibhasa* also uses more colloquialisms, phrases, and
idioms than does *Sadhubhasa*, which uses spoken forms from the formal
Sanskrit and Islamic literary traditions.

Many linguists believe that the use of traditional Sanskrit words is a
defining characteristic of *Sadhubhasa*. Having been the language of the
elite for centuries, it stands to reason that the academic language of Bengal
should be influenced by Sanskrit.

A group of boys learn to read.

Other linguists believe the influence is predominantly Persio-Arabic, which is evident in the borrowing of Persio-Arabic words, the recreation of Islamic ideas, and the use of similes and metaphors in Bengali.

Chaltibhasa first became commonly used during the early years of World War I. Today it has almost entirely replaced *Sadhubhasa* in common speech. Nevertheless *Sadhubhasa* is still taught in schools as the traditional style. There are also stylistic differences between the different social classes of *Chaltibhasa* speakers—just as in the English language of Great Britain there are regional and socioeconomic variations in grammar, vocabulary, and pronunciation.

There are distinct variations, for example, between the Bengali spoken by an educated person from Dhaka and that of a factory worker from Khulna. However, they can still understand each other. The distinction between *Sadhubhasa* and "prestigious" and "common" *Chaltibhasa* can best be compared to the distinction between Shakespearean, aristocratic, and working-class forms of English in Great Britain.

THE SCRIPT

The Bengali script is one of many North Indian scripts derived from Sanskrit. These scripts are midway between alphabets and syllables, and consist of symbols that represent a consonant and a vowel sound. Some vowel sounds are written as separate symbols, and these are attached somewhere on the consonant, sometimes even before it.

Indian scripts have a unique feature called a "consonant conjunct." This is a process where two consonants that occur together, without a vowel dividing them, are orthographically conjoined into one special letter.

A bilingual sign in Cox's Bazar. While there are relatively few individual letters in North Indian scripts, such as Bengali, there are possibilities for a very large number of consonant conjuncts.

THE MEDIA

Bangladesh has over 1,000 newspapers and magazines, including more than 100 daily newspapers. Major Bengali newspapers include *Dainik Ittefaq* (with a circulation of about 200,000), *Dainik Inquilab* (180,000), *Dainik Janakantha* (100,000), and *Sangbad* (73,000), all published in Dhaka.

The other cities also have their own newspapers, for example, *Dainik Sphulinga* (published in Jessore, with a circulation of about 14,000), *Azadi* (Chittagong, 13,000), and *Dainik Rupashi Bangla* (Comilla, 8,000). Bangladesh's low literacy rate, however, means that many Bangladeshis do not read these newspapers.

Bangladesh also has a number of English language dailies. These include the *Bangladesh Observer* (circulation: 43,000), *The Bangladesh Times* (35,000), the *Daily Star* (30,000)—all published in Dhaka—and the Khulna-based *Daily Tribune* (22,000). English, a legacy of decades of British colonial rule, is widely spoken in urban areas, and many shops and business offices have signs in both Bengali and English. English is also used for some government and legal matters.

Radio Bangladesh and Bangladesh Television were both established in 1971. These organizations merged in 1984 to form the government-controlled National Broadcasting Authority. Radio Bangladesh transmits throughout Bangladesh through its regional stations in Dhaka, Chittagong, Khulna, Rajshahi, Rangpur, and Sylhet. It also transmits to South Asia, the Middle East, Africa, and western Europe in Bengali, English, Arabic, Hindi, Nepalese, and Urdu, via its shortwave station in Dhaka.

Bangladesh Television, which started color transmissions in 1980, provides two channels that are available all over the country. However, outside of Dhaka, very few people own television sets, so it is a relatively underutilized medium for communication.

Left: **Movie and election posters vie for attention.**

Opposite: **In Bangladesh the newspaper has many uses, including the wrapping of food. Newspapers in the country have a combined circulation of only about two million. In a country of 123 million people, this reflects a low literacy rate.**

ARTS

ALTHOUGH BANGLADESH HAS A RICH TRADITION IN THE ARTS, going as far back as the first millennium A.D., the country's harsh weather has destroyed many of the ancient pre-Islamic artworks. Nevertheless, a few temples and religious monuments that display the traditions of these cultures still stand today.

They provide compelling evidence that a rich and continuous tradition in bronze sculpture, mostly depicting Buddhist and Hindu deities, once thrived here. Stone sculptures dating as early as the second century A.D., believed to have been decorations in temples or other large buildings, have also been found. The relatively large number of Buddhist sculptures discovered reflect the former dominance of Buddhism in Bangladesh. After the 12th century, production of such sculptures declined sharply, corresponding with the Muslim invasion from the north.

Opposite and left: **The art and tradition of carving have been passed on to the younger generation of artists.**

A wall mosaic promotes Bangladeshi nationalism.

ISLAMIC ART

Islam prohibits Muslim artists from representing human figures in artwork, based on the doctrine that only Allah may create life. Instead, Islamic art is characterized by ornate calligraphy and arabesque designs. Passages of the Koran are written elaborately and colorfully decorated with intertwining leaves and flowing patterns.

CONTEMPORARY ART

The contemporary works of modern Bangladeshi artists reflect recent trends on the international art scene. Abstract and representative works are produced in sculpture, tapestry, engraving, and painting. Several Bangladeshi artists have gained international recognition for their work, including Zainul Abedin, noted for his sketches of the 1943 Bengali famine.

NO ORDINARY CANVAS

The streets of Dhaka are filled with some 140,000 rickshaws, which are the principal means of transport for most Dhakans. Since the 1930s rickshaws have symbolized the daily life of Bangladeshis. In the 1970s Bangladeshi artists began to use rickshaws as a way to display their work.

This trend became so popular that today the painted rickshaw is a cultural phenomenon. Rickshaw owners commission artists to paint vivid, colorful murals all over the rickshaw, including the hood, back, seats, and wheels.

ARCHITECTURE

The evolution of Bangladeshi architecture reflects the attitudes of the ruling powers of the time. For example, the Hindu and Buddhist temples of the pre-Islamic Indian era followed their respective traditional styles. The distinctive arches and domes that have long been recognized as fundamental characteristics of mosques were introduced at the time of the Moghul invasion. Sometimes the styles crossed over, so that Hindu temples were influenced by Islamic architecture, and integrated Islamic features with traditional Hindu elements, such as the terracotta decorations.

European styles of architecture first appeared in churches in Dhaka in and around the 1800s, and a unique hybrid of Moghul and European designs gradually developed. Only since the 1960s has a really strong Western influence been felt. Most present-day houses are simply constructed out of wood and bamboo or mud-brick and thatch. Modern commercial architecture is similar to Western styles.

Islamic architecture in a Chittagong mosque.

PERFORMING ARTS

The performing arts of Bangladesh, despite recent developments in theater, movies, television, and radio, remain very much centered in the village folk culture. Outdoor stagings of drama, music, and poetry recitations are often seen in the villages, where the arts are most alive and vibrant. This is the principal way that the traditions are continued.

DANCE

Dance forms are almost entirely from Hindu or tribal traditions, as dance is not used as a mode of artistic expression in Islam. Hindu dance was originally a prayer, and is still used as such. The classical dance that is popular in Bangladesh today is a combination of Western ballet forms and Hindu styles.

Folk dances take various forms, but the seasons and events of rural life are themes in almost all of them. For example, a dance called *moni puri* ("MOH-nee POO-ree") is a celebration by the entire community that takes place on the first full moon night after the harvest. The dances of the Chittagong hill tribes show distinct influences from neighboring Burma.

Hindu dancers in a performance in Dhaka.

KIRTAN

The Hindu prayer dance-cum-song is called *kirtan* ("KEER-tahn"). Arms are raised above the head or hands are held together in a prayer position. The way in which the dancer moves and touches the ground with his or her feet is believed to stimulate the *chakras* ("CHAH-krah"), or the centers of energy in the body.

At the same time, the dancer chants and sings, often Sanskritic phrases which are praises to the gods. The chants, such as "Hare Krishna" and "Babanam Kevalam," are all essentially different ways of expressing the idea of eternal love. The resonance produced in the voice through chanting is said to inspire the same physical feeling that is achieved through meditation.

MUSIC

Bangladeshi music consists of three main categories: the traditional, classical music of the Indian style; folk music; and a modern style influenced by contemporary Western "pop" music. The main melody is usually carried by vocal expression and is supported by instruments.

Sitars ("sit-AHRS," a classical Indian stringed instrument), violins, and flutes are favored instruments. Bamboo flutes are especially popular in rural areas, where the soft, lingering songs of herdsmen and boatmen are loved. *Baia* ("BY-ah") and *tabla* ("tah-BLA") drums are used in concerts and for classical music and the *dhole* ("DOL"), or country drum, is a common village instrument.

Western-style popular music began to strongly influence Bangladeshi music in the early 1970s. Several recording studios were established in Dhaka, which produced many folk and tribal songs and also thousands of pop-style songs about national heroes and martyrs that were written after independence.

DRAMA

Little drama was produced by Bangladeshis prior to the independence movement against the British. With the rise of nationalism in the 1930s, both Muslims and Hindus began to write plays, principally on the theme of nationalism. Nevertheless, there was little in the way of dramatic productions until after 1971, when several companies began presenting plays in Dhaka and amateur groups sprang up in Chittagong.

Dramatic performances have, however, never attracted as wide a following as movies. The exceptions are the village folk plays. These *jatra* ("JA-trah") plays are by far the most distinctive form of Bangladeshi drama, preserving folk tales in comedy, tragedy, and melodrama.

A traveling village troupe makes its way across the countryside.

They are usually outdoor productions, complete with sets, costumes, and makeup, and performed by local actors, singers, dancers, and musicians. Another popular dramatic activity is the *kabiagn* ("KA-byne"), a poetry contest in which two people debate in impromptu verse. Each contestant is accompanied by a few musical instruments and a vocal chorus that repeats the contestant's lines.

The *Esraj*

The *esraj* ("EHZ-rahj") is a traditional Bengali instrument. It has a short, waisted chamber and a long, broad neck. The player places the base in his or her lap, holding it vertically with the neck resting on his or her left shoulder. The four strings are played with a bow and by pressing along the frets, similar to playing the violin. The soft, mellow tone of the *esraj* can be hauntingly beautiful, whether played solo or in a group, or as an accompaniment to vocal music.

Water jars are potters' main products. Pots painted with brightly colored geometric, floral, and animal motifs are made by many potters for pleasure.

FOLK CRAFT

POTTERY With some 680 villages devoted entirely to the manufacture of pots, pottery is the most common art form in Bangladesh. The pots are made on wheels and in molds, by both men and women.

TEXTILES Bengali textiles have for centuries been regarded as of superior quality. Before British rule, fine muslin was made in the Dhaka region and exported as far as Europe. According to folklore, the muslin was so fine and transparent that it took seven layers to conceal the body, and eleven yards (10 m) could be wadded in one hand.

Despite British discouragement of the art, a high level of skill in weaving has persisted throughout the years, both at the textile mills and at individual looms. Bangladeshi cotton and silk *saris* are prized all over the subcontinent for the exquisite quality of the fabric, the colorful and intricate, often kaleidoscopic, floral and geometric designs, and the delicate embroidery.

LITERATURE

"At heart, all Bangladeshis are poets."

—Anon

THE BLANK AGE No written records of Bengali literature exist from the period A.D. 1200–1350, and so this time is often referred to as the Blank or Dark Age.

MEDIEVAL LITERATURE A notable feature of medieval Bengali literature is that it was entirely verse. Mostly centered on religious themes, lyrical poems and long eulogistic poems—sometimes consisting of tens of thousands of lines—appear throughout the period. Not all had religious themes, though. A large number of poems also focused on rural life and politics.

Like Tagore, Shamsur Rahman, a leading modern-day poet, produces his works in Bengali.

MODERN LITERATURE The British colonization of the Indian sub-continent greatly influenced Bengali literature. European styles of education, Christianity, and the introduction of the English language all played a vital role in shaping the Bengali literary style.

In the late 1800s several events sparked a wave of literary production. First, the Bengali script, which had been slowly evolving, developed into the form that exists today, thus giving Bengali writers a truly Bengali tool to utilize. Second, Bengali nationalism emerged. These two factors were the impetus for a cultural renaissance, in which Bengali identity became the dominating theme. The poet Rabindranath Tagore, who won a Nobel Prize in literature, chose to write all his works in Bengali, even after studying in England for several years.

POETICALLY POLITICAL

Many poems written by Bengali poets are based on the themes of nationalism, independence, and lamented war heroes. Here are two poems by the two most famous Bengali writers, Rabindranath Tagore (left) and Kazi Nazrul Islam.

Tagore achieved international fame for his 1,000 poems, two dozen plays, eight novels, eight volumes of short stories, 2,000 songs (for which he composed the music as well as the lyrics), paintings, lectures, and a mass of prose on literary, religious, social, and political topics. Islam earned the popular nickname "Rebel Poet" for his outspoken, patriotic writings, which were enormously influential in the liberation struggle.

Where The Mind Is Without Fear

Where the mind is without fear and the head is held high
Where knowledge is free
Where the world has not been broken up into fragments
By narrow domestic walls
Where words come out from the depth of truth
Where tireless striving stretches its arms towards perfection
Where the clear stream of reason has not lost its way
Into the dreary desert sand of dead habit
Where the mind is led forward by thee
Into ever-widening thought and action
Into that heaven of freedom, my Father, let my country awake.

—Rabindranath Tagore

Thieves and Robbers

Who calls you a robber, my friend? Who calls you a thief?
All around the robbers beat their drums and thieves rule.
Who is the Daniel that sits in judgement over thieves and robbers?
Is there any in the world that is not an exploiter?
O Supreme judge, hold high your scepter,
For the great are great today only by robbing the weak.
The greater the robbery and theft, the cheating and the exploitation
The higher the status in the modern world of nations!
Palaces rise built with the congealed blood of subject peoples,
Capitalists run their factories by destroying a million hearths.
What diabolical machine is fed by human flesh?
Live men and women go in but come out like pressed sugar cane.
The factories squeeze the manhood out of millions,
And fill the millionaire's cup of wine and jars of gold.
The money lender grows potbellied on the food that the hungry need,
The landlord ruins the poor's home to drive his coach and four.
The merchant mind has turned the world into a brothel house,
Sin and Satan are its cup bearers and sing a song of greed.
Man has lost food and health and life and hope and speech,
Bankrupt, he rushes toward secure destruction.
There is hardly any way of escape,
For all around are trenches dug by the greed of gold.

The whole world is a prison and robbers are the guards.
Thieves have their brotherhood, cheats their comradeship.
Who calls you a robber, my friend? Who says you steal?
You have only taken a few coins or cups,
But you have not stabbed man in the heart!
You are not inhuman though you may be a thief,
Like Ratnakar, you can still become Valmiki if only you meet a real man!

—Kazi Nazrul Islam

I, the eternal rebel,
Shall rest in quiet
only when I find
The sky and the
air free
Of the piteous
groans of the
oppressed.

—Kazi Nazrul Islam

LEISURE

IN A COUNTRY RANKED AS ONE OF THE POOREST in the world, Bangladeshis have become adept at recognizing and enjoying the simple pleasures of life during their leisure hours.

A wedding or a birth in a village, for example, is always an occasion for relatives, friends, and neighbors to get together. Here they can eat, drink, catch up on the latest family news and happenings, and renew ties with each other. Similarly an outdoor musical drama or performance never fails to attract crowds eager for good entertainment.

Sports and games also offer hours of pleasure, especially for boys. An impromptu game of soccer requires only an empty plot of land and a ball. Watching television, listening to the radio, and going to the movies are popular pastimes for those who can afford a television or radio set, or the price of a movie ticket.

Opposite: **A vendor in Dhaka sells colorful balloons at a fair ground.**

Left: **A competition to pick the best prize bulls draws an enthusiastic crowd of spectators.**

In Bangladeshi society, women and men do not socialize together. Women do their socializing as they perform household tasks.

SOCIALIZING

Men do a great deal of socializing in public places. After prayers at the mosque, men often visit a tea shop and sit together, chatting and drinking sweet tea, for several hours. Women do most of their socializing in the courtyard of their home, while performing their household tasks. They may weave or prepare food while they chat and gossip. Women visit each others' homes as well.

Bangladeshis can be very generous hosts. No effort or expense is spared to demonstrate the esteem in which a guest is held, and a small meal is always given to guests. A hostess will even prepare an impromptu meal for visitors who drop in unexpectedly. Dinner guests may be asked to arrive at 8 p.m. so that they have time for conversation before the meal is served. And for special dinner parties, hosts sometimes go to the extent of arranging musical entertainment.

SPORTS AND GAMES

Sports and games are extremely popular in Bangladesh. Children can often be observed playing soccer or cricket in quiet village streets. Many people enjoy chess as a recreational and competitive activity. *Kabaddi* ("KAH-bah-dee") is a popular, and physical, indigenous sport, in which teams of six try to capture members of the opposing team. But the most popular sport in Bangladesh is undoubtedly soccer, which is played and supported passionately. Cricket, badminton, field hockey, tennis, swimming, and track and field also have avid followings.

Bangladesh competes in many international sports events, including the Olympics, Commonwealth, Asian, and South Asian Federation games. In the 1980 Asian Youth Soccer Tournament hosted by Bangladesh, the home team defeated some of their more fancied opponents to emerge runners-up. More often, however, the act of participating at international events is already a source of pride and achievement for all Bangladeshis.

Two boys play badminton on a Dhaka street. Badminton has been a competition sport at the Olympics since 1992, with the best players coming from China, Indonesia, and Denmark.

A movie poster promises entertainment and excitement. Bangladesh has about 1,000 movie theaters with a total of over 500,000 seats.

MOVIES, TELEVISION, AND RADIO

Movies are a popular form of entertainment in Bangladesh. The country has produced its own films since 1956; today over 100 feature films are produced annually. Despite the fact that most are long melodramas about the struggle for independence with mediocre acting and production quality, the movies attract an enthusiastic audience. In recent years efforts have been made to improve standards.

Few Bangladeshis own television sets, so while they enjoy watching television, not many have the luxury of being able to. In urban households, only 7% own a television set; in rural households less than 1% do. The two channels offer a variety of locally produced dramas and news programs as well as foreign shows, including American soap operas and sitcoms. Many Bangladeshis also enjoy listening to the radio, but again, only a minority own radios—29% in the cities and 13% elsewhere. A number of stations play music of varying styles, and read passages from the Koran and other scriptures.

CHILDHOOD PURSUITS

Like their counterparts the world over, Bangladeshi children have little difficulty finding ways to amuse themselves. Lack of money is seldom an obstacle, as simple toys can be made using whatever material is available and games can be as basic as playing hide-and-seek. Sports are also popular with many older children.

Yet many Bangladeshi children have little time to play. Young girls who do not attend school are put to work in the home, helping their mother and other female relatives with the household chores. Many children from poor families are also sent to work in factories and markets or placed in other employment to earn vital income to support their parents and siblings. Such work is often poorly paid, with long hours and tough working conditions.

A boy with his kite—using a little bit of ingenuity for a lot of fun.

FESTIVALS

ALTHOUGH PREDOMINANTLY MUSLIM, Bangladesh also celebrates festivals for Hindus, Buddhists, and Christians as well as secular events.

MUSLIM FESTIVALS

Perhaps the most important event on the Islamic calendar is Ramadan, the period of fasting. Although Ramadan is not a festival in the true sense, the *iftar* ("IF-tah") celebrations that go on in the evenings when the fast is broken have all the attributes of a festival. A fortnight before Ramadan begins, alms and sweets are given to the poor.

Eid al-Fitr ("ID al-FIT-er") is a three-day festival celebrated immediately after the end of Ramadan. Bangladeshis eat special foods and socialize all night long. Most schools, shops, and offices are closed during the festival, and many people take vacation trips.

Opposite: **An elephant and its rider join in the Victory Day celebrations.**

Left: **Spectators at the Dhaka stadium await the start of the next event on the Victory Day program of festivities.**

A Muharram procession commemorates the martyrdom of the Prophet Mohammed's grandson Hussein.

THE RULES OF RAMADAN

A number of rules must be observed during Ramadan. Certain acts nullify the fast; if a person breaks the fast by performing one of these acts he or she must make up for the lost time. Actions that nullify the fast include:

- Eating or drinking *intentionally* between dawn and sunset. If a Muslim eats or drinks unintentionally, forgetting that he or she is fasting, it is forgiven because it is said that Allah gave the food or drink to the person.

- Sexual intercourse

- Intentional vomiting

- Injections containing nourishment (unless for medical purposes)

- Poor intentions—for example, intending to break the fast or not intending to start is a sin, even if the intention is not acted on.

- Involuntary actions, such as bleeding due to menstruation or childbirth.

OTHER RELIGIOUS FESTIVALS

Hindus celebrate the Festival of Colors at the beginning of March. During this festival, the participants throw colored water and powder on each other, and caste and social restrictions on both men and women are momentarily ignored. The festival for Durga Puja ("DERG-ah POO-jah"), a Hindu goddess, is celebrated in October. Statues of the goddess riding a lion, with her 10 hands holding 10 different weapons, are placed in Hindu temples. Buddhists celebrate the birth of the Buddha, and Christians celebrate Christmas and Easter.

SECULAR EVENTS

SHAHEED DIBOSH (MARTYRS' DAY) Celebrated on February 21, this day commemorates the death of four martyrs who were killed when Pakistani police opened fire on a procession protesting the decision to make Urdu the national language of East and West Pakistan.

INDEPENDENCE DAY On March 26, 1971, Bangladesh declared its independence from Pakistan, sparking off a nine-month war. Independence Day celebrates the Bangladeshis' fight for nationalism.

BENGALI NEW YEAR Falls on April 14.

***BIJOY DIBOSH* (VICTORY DAY)** This festival celebrates the day Bangladesh was finally liberated from Pakistan. Victory Day, December 16, marks the end of the war of independence and the birth of Bangladesh as a free nation.

Girls in traditional dress in a Victory Day procession.

CALENDAR OF BANGLADESHI HOLIDAYS

Muslim festivals fall on different dates each year because they are based on the Islamic lunar calendar. The following are some of the major religious and secular festivals celebrated in Bangladesh:

Martyrs' Day	February 21
Independence Day	March 26
Bengali New Year	April 14
May Day	May 1
Durga Puja	October
National Solidarity Day	November 7
Victory Day	December 16
Christmas	December 25
Eid al-Fitr	varies
Eid al-Azha	varies
Muharram	varies
Prophet Mohammed's Birthday	varies
Buddha's Birthday	varies

FOOD

THE CUISINE OF BANGLADESH, like that of its neighbors on the Indian subcontinent, has been influenced by the many conquerors who have passed through its land over the centuries. As a result, the cuisine that has evolved is representative of the South Asia region.

The Moghul rulers have perhaps left the most lasting impression, and even today some of Bangladesh's food is derived from this heritage. The most visible examples of such food include *kebabs* ("KUH-babs," chunks of meat marinated in spices and grilled on skewers) and *koftas* ("KOF-tah," meatballs). These foods are common also to Iran and northern India, regions that were once part of the extensive Moghul empire that reached its peak during the 17th century.

Opposite: **Preparing the ingredients for a curry.**

Left: **Choosing the best fowls at a poultry market in Dhaka.**

Sacks of rice and other food in a Dhaka shop. Non-Muslim farming families with excess rice sometimes brew beer or distill liquor with it.

RICE

Rice is the staple of the Bangladeshi diet and is served with almost every meal. The poor eat just plain rice with salt and pepper. The rice is prepared by boiling or by frying in butter or oil. When there is a shortage of rice, gruel or, reluctantly, wheat is eaten as a substitute.

Fish is a common side dish and provides most of the protein in the Bangladeshi diet. Meat, on the other hand, is reserved almost exclusively for festive occasions. Cattle, deer, goat, and chicken are commonly eaten. Every edible part of the animal is used, including the organs, and bones are boiled for stock. Domestic animals are the main source of meat, but these may be supplemented with hunted animals, such as wood pigeons, wild boars, iguanas, and large cats.

Chittagong fruit vendors
with bananas and other
fruit.

FRUIT AND VEGETABLES

A wide variety of tropical fruit grows bountifully in Bangladesh. Mangoes, jackfruit, coconuts, bananas, and many other fruit are eaten fresh or form the basis of many desserts. The availability of some fruit varies seasonally, but bananas, jackfruit, and papaya are almost always available in low-lying villages. Mandarin oranges are also becoming more common in the markets.

Wild limes, which grow in the hills, are also a favorite with Bangladeshis. Most homes in the countryside have vegetable gardens that yield a ready supply of fresh vegetables for the family. In between harvests, leaves and roots, such as bamboo shoots and banana stalks, are gathered from the wild for the cooking pot.

Above: **A typical family meal. Like many other Asians, Bangladeshis eat with their hand, usually the right one.**

Opposite: **A snack vendor in Chittagong awaits customers.**

MEALS

Breakfast is served very early, particularly in Muslim families. Men get up at dawn to pray, while the women prepare a breakfast of rice and milk and perhaps some fruit. A fairly large lunch is eaten at midday, before the sun gets too hot.

The first time that the family is able to relax together is at the evening meal, which is usually served quite late, at 9:30 or 10 p.m. The family gathers on the verandah and sits on a bamboo mat, usually on the floor. The mother of the household serves food on individual plates to everybody. The meal does not begin until everyone has washed their hands. The evening meal usually consists of rice, spicy lentil, or *dahl* ("DAHL"), vegetables, and a little fish.

SHEMAI (SWEET VERMICELLI)

Here is a recipe for a popular Bangladeshi dessert, *shemai* ("SHA-my"):

3 tablespoons butter
2 handfuls fine vermicelli
4 cups milk
1 handful raisins

sliced almonds (optional)
1 tablespoon sugar
1 pint (2$^1/_2$ cups) whipping cream

Melt butter in a pot. Break vermicelli into 3-inch (7$^1/_2$ cm) pieces. Over low heat stir vermicelli into the butter until it turns light brown.

Pour in the milk and stir over medium heat until it boils. Put in the raisins, almonds, and sugar.

Continue to cook on low heat for 10 minutes. Add cream and cook for several more minutes. Remove from heat and allow to cool. Serve cold.

KITCHENS

Rural *baris* usually have a small shed that is not as well built as a sleeping room. This is designated as the kitchen. An interesting feature of Bangladeshi kitchens is the stove, which is built into the mud floor. Even in the more affluent homes with brick walls and cement floors for the other rooms, the kitchen retains the mud floor. There may also be a built-in mud stove in the courtyard for open-air cooking during fair weather.

Cooking utensils quickly become covered in soot from the stoves and so need to be regularly cleaned by rubbing them with ash and coconut husks. Utensils that are found in most kitchens include a grinding stone, round-bottomed earthenware pots, a winnowing basket, and a curved cutting edge fixed to a wooden base. Only very wealthy homes can afford kitchens equipped with modern appliances such as microwave ovens.

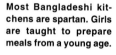

Most Bangladeshi kitchens are spartan. Girls are taught to prepare meals from a young age.

FORBIDDEN FOODS

The Bangladeshi diet has been influenced by the restrictions of the country's main religions. Muslims, for example, do not consume pork or alcohol as Islam forbids it. Similarly, Hindu Bangladeshis do not eat beef, as the cow is considered a sacred animal by Hindu teachings. The relative absence of alcoholic beverages means Bangladesh is very much a country of soft drinks, with the ubiquitous Pepsi and Coca-Cola evident even in the villages.

INTERNATIONAL FOODS

A modest variety of international cuisines, including Western food, can be found at major hotels in the larger cities. In addition to several Chinese restaurants, Dhaka has Thai, Korean, and Japanese restaurants.

A cook prepares the food for the day's business.

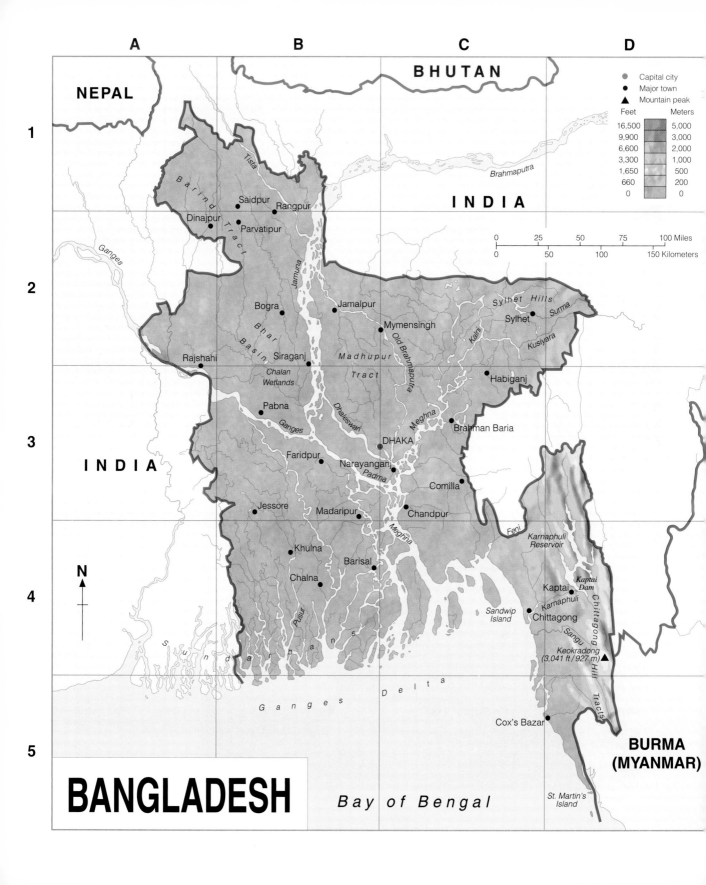

BANGLADESH

NEPAL

BHUTAN

INDIA

INDIA

BURMA (MYANMAR)

Bay of Bengal

	Legend
●	Capital city
●	Major town
▲	Mountain peak

Feet	Meters
16,500	5,000
9,900	3,000
6,600	2,000
3,300	1,000
1,650	500
660	200
0	0

0 25 50 75 100 Miles
0 50 100 150 Kilometers

N

Barind Tract

Saidpur
Rangpur
Dinajpur
Parvatipur

Tista

Jamuna

Brahmaputra

Bogra
Jamalpur
Mymensingh
Sylhet

Sylhet Hills
Surma
Kusiyara

Bhar Basin

Siraganj
Rajshahi

Chalan Wetlands

Madhupur Tract

Old Brahmaputra

Kalni

Habiganj

Pabna

Ganges
Dhaleswari
Meghna

DHAKA

Brahman Baria

Faridpur
Narayanganj

Padma

Comilla

Jessore
Madaripur
Chandpur

Khulna
Chalna
Barisal

Meghna

Feni

Karnaphuli Reservoir

Kaptai Dam

Kaptai

Karnaphuli

Sandwip Island
Chittagong

Chittagong Hill Tracts

Sangu

Keokradong
(3,041 ft / 927 m) ▲

Pusur

S u n d a r b a n s

G a n g e s   D e l t a

Cox's Bazar

St. Martin's Island

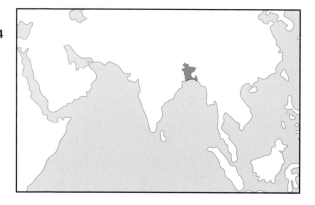

QUICK NOTES

AREA
55,598 square miles
(144,000 square km)

POPULATION
123 million (1996 estimate)

CAPITAL
Dhaka

OFFICIAL NAME
People's Republic of Bangladesh

OFFICIAL LANGUAGE
Bengali

HIGHEST POINT
Keokradong (3,041 ft / 927 m)

MAJOR LAKE
Kaptai Lake

OFFICIAL RELIGION
Islam

RIVERS
Ganges, Brahmaputra, Jamuna, Padma

NATIONAL ANIMAL
The Bengal tiger

CLIMATE
Tropical monsoon with average temperatures
of 67°F (19°C) from October to March, rising to
84°F (29°C) between May and September

MAJOR CITIES
Chittagong, Khulna, Rajshahi, Mymensingh,
Sylhet

NATIONAL FLAG
Green with a red disc to the left of center

CURRENCY
The Bangladeshi taka
1 taka = 100 poisha
US$1 = 43 taka

MAIN EXPORTS
Ready-made garments, jute, fish and shrimps,
hides, skins, leather, tea

MAJOR IMPORTS
Textile yarn and fabrics, machinery and transport
equipment, petroleum, chemicals

POLITICAL LEADERS
Sheikh Mujibur Rahman—prime minister from
    1972 to 1975
Mohammad Ershad—prime minister from 1982
    to 1983, president from 1983 to 1990
Begum Khaleda Zia—prime minister from 1991
    to 1996

LEADERS IN THE ARTS
Rabindranath Tagore, Kazi Nazrul Islam

ANNIVERSARIES
Martyrs' Day (February 21)
Independence Day (March 26)
Victory Day (December 16)

GLOSSARY

atur ghar ("ah-TOO ghor")
Birthing room—a room in the house designated to be the natal home for 40 days after birth.

bari ("BAH-ree")
Rural Bangladeshi home.

Chaltibhasa ("CHAHL-tee-bah-sah")
Informal style of Bengali now used by most Bangladeshis in common speech. Developed chiefly during the 20th century.

dhole ("DOL")
Country drum, a common village instrument.

goli ("GOH-lee")
Area in the home used by men for socializing.

hajj ("hahj")
Pilgrimage to Mecca, the holy city of Islam. All Muslims should try to perform the *hajj* at least once in their life, if they can.

jatra ("JA-trah")
Village folk play.

jhum ("juhm")
Swidden agriculture—practiced mainly by the hill tribes of the Chittagong Hill Tracts.

kanta ("KAN-tah")
Garden at the rear of the home.

lungi ("LOONG-gee")
Sarong-like cloth worn by men.

milad ("MI-lahd")
Religious gathering where the life of the Prophet Mohammed is discussed and prayers are offered.

nagra ("NAH-grah")
Traditional decorative slippers.

Ramadan ("RUM-ah-dahn")
Period of fasting required of all Muslims.

Sadhubhasa ("SAH-DOO-bah-sah")
Traditional, literary style of Bengali, based on the Middle Bengali of the 16th century. Still taught in schools as the traditional style.

salat ("sah-LAHT")
Daily prayer, five times a day, by Muslims.

shagatom ("SHAH-gah-tom")
"Welcome," in Bengali.

shahadah ("shah-HAH-dah")
Testimonial prayer stating the central belief of Islam—that there is no god but Allah.

shemai ("SHA-my")
Sweet vermicelli, a popular dessert.

sherwani ("sher-WAH-nee")
Ankle-length, collarless jacket worn by men on formal occasions.

zakat ("zah-KAHT")
The giving of alms to the poor.

BIBLIOGRAPHY

Banu, U.A.B. Razia Akter. *Islam in Bangladesh.* Leiden, New York, 1992.

Chakravarti, S.R. & Narain, Virendra. *Bangladesh.* New Dehli: South Asian Publishers, 1986.

Novak, James J. *Reflections on the Water.* Bloomington: Indiana University Press, 1993.

The Chittagong Hill Tracts: Militarization, Oppression and the Hill Tribes. London: Anti-Slavery Society, 1984.

West Asia on a Shoestring. Victoria, Australia: Lonely Planet Publications, 1990.

INDEX

INDEX

INDEX

PICTURE CREDITS